# STEPS
# TO PERSONAL
# REVIVAL

# ORDER INFORMATION

**USA, Canada**
*Roy Rugless*  
Email: pastorug@bellsouth.net  
Phone: (256) 520 - 7077

*Dennis Smith*  
Booklets in English  
smith06515@msn.com

**Philippines:**
*Allan D. Faina*, Email: allan@lightingtheworld.org  
Address: SDA church, Fidela Herrera Subd, Bgy. Santol, Tanza, Cavite-4108 Philippines  
Phones: (63) 926 054 1175

**Australien:**
*Colin Hone*  
Booklets in English  
colin.hone@murrayhone.com.au

**Germany and abroad:**
*Wertvoll leben*, Im Kiesel 3, D-73635 Rudersberg/Württ.  
www.wertvollleben.com, Email: info@wertvollleben.com  
Phone: +49 (0)7183 / 309 98 47

**Austria:**
*TOP Life Wegweiser-Verlag*, Prager Str.287, A-1210 Wien/Vienna  
www.toplife-center.com, Email: info@wegweiser-verlag.at  
Phone +43 [0] 13199301-0

**Austria and Germany:**
*Adventist Book Center*, Bogenhofen, A-4963 St.Peter/Hart  
www.adventistbookcenter.at, Email: info@adventistbookcenter.at  
Phone +43-(0)-2294000

**Switzerland:**
*Advent-Verlag*, Leissigenstr. 17, CH-3704 Krattigen  
www.av-buchshop.ch, Email: info@adventverlag.ch  
Phone +41 33 654 1065

# Steps
## TO PERSONAL
## Revival

*Being filled with the
Holy Spirit*

HELMUT HAUBEIL

# TABLE OF CONTENTS

# TABLE OF CONTENTS

## OUR LORD HIMSELF
## HAS GIVEN THE COMMAND [1]

# LET YOURSELVES
# BE CONSISTENTLY AND
# REPEATEDLY FILLED ANEW
# WITH THE SPIRIT! [2]

1   E.G. White, Mount of Blessing, MB 20.3 (egwwritings.org)
2   Johannes Mager, Auf den Spuren des Heiligen Geistes (Lüneburg, 1999), Seite 101

# STEPS TO PERSONAL REVIVAL

*Filled with the Holy Spirit*

*Why was it that I was suddenly intensively occupied with the matter of "Life in the Holy Ghost"?*

On August 14, 2011, when I was in Kandergrund in the Bernese High-lands in Switzerland an important connection became very clear to me. I recognized a spiritual cause for why we are losing part of our youth. I was very shocked. I thought of my children and grandchildren. Since then I have been intensively occupied with this subject.

> *Now I believe that the same spiritual cause is behind many of our problems; specifically the personal problems, in the local churches and the world-wide church. It is the lack of the Holy Spirit.*

If this is the cause, then we should urgently address this issue. If the cause can be eliminated or considerably reduced, then many pro-blems will become superfluous or will be resolved.

## What others have to say about this deficiency:

- **EMIL BRUNNER,** *an Evangelical reformed theologian, wrote that the Holy Ghost "has always more or less been the stepchild of theology."*[1]

- **D. MARTIN LLOYD-JONES:** *"If I may give my honest opinion, then there is no topic on biblical belief that has been so neglected in the past or present as the topic of the Holy Ghost…. I am sure that this is the cause for the weakness of the evangelical faith."*[2]

- **LEROY E. FROOM:** *"I am convinced that the lack of the Holy Spirit is our worst problem."*[3]

- **DWIGHT NELSON:** *"Our church has to the point of exhaustion developed admirable forms, plans and programs, but if we don't finally admit to our spiritual bankruptcy [lack of the Holy Spirit], which has overtaken many of us ministers and leaders, then we will never be able to get out of our Pro-Forma-Christianity."*[4]

- **GARRIE F. WILLIAMS:** *"It seems that the Holy Spirit largely plays a minor role, if at all, in the daily lives of many Adventists and in church life. And yet this is the foundation for a joyful, attractive and fruit-bearing life in Christ."*[5]

- **A. W. TOZER:** *"If the Holy Ghost were taken away from our church today, 95% of what we do would continue and no one would notice the difference. If the Holy Ghost had withdrawn from the early church, then 95% of what they were doing would have stopped and everyone would have noticed the difference."*[6]

· To start with, we want to take a short look at a few references that the Lord Jesus made about the Holy Ghost.

1   Johannes Mager, *Auf den Spuren des Heiligen Geistes*, (Lüneburg, 1999), Cover
2   D. Martin Lloyd-Jones, *Vollmacht, Telos-Taschenbuch* Nr. 385, Marburg 1984, p. 72
3   E.G. White, *The Coming of the Comforter* (Hagerstown, 1949), p. 94
4   Editor Helmut Haubeil, *Missionsbrief Nr. 34 (Bad Aibling, 2011)*, Seite 3
5   Garrie F. Williams, *How to be filled by the Holy Spirit and know it* (Lüneburg, 2007), Cover
6   Dr. S. Joseph Kidder, *Anleitung zum geistlichen Leben* (Andrews University), PPP slide 2

# CHAPTER 1

# JESUS' MOST PRECIOUS GIFT

## WHAT DID JESUS TEACH ABOUT THE HOLY SPIRIT?

*Are you acquainted with Jesus' most powerful message?*

### A few of the first personal testimonies:

**Back to our "first love":** A sister wrote to me: My friend and I are currently studying the "40 Days" book for the third time alternating with the booklet "Steps to Personal Revival". Before we discovered this material our faith experience and prayer life wasn't what it once had been. **We longed to find our "first love" again.** We have found it! We thank God with our whole hearts. It is so wonderful how our loving God answers prayers and that He reveals how His Spirit is working – on us and on the people we are praying for. M.S.

**Jesus entered our lives:** Another person wrote about these books: "...they have become a great and long-awaited blessing in my life. Just like many other church members and a sister from our church have experienced, something was always missing in our faith experience and now we have had the privilege of experiencing how **Jesus has entered our lives** and has begun to change us. He is still working on us and step by step is drawing us closer to Him." S.K.

**Did Jesus' disciples ask themselves: How can Jesus exercise such a great influence?** Was it connected with His prayer life? That is why they asked Him: *"Lord, teach us to pray."* Jesus responded to their request.

His prayer lesson in Luke 11:1-13 has three parts: The Lord's Prayer, the parable of the friend coming at midnight and as a climax the continual request for the Holy Ghost.

In the parable (verses 5-8) visitors arrive at a man's home late in the evening and he **has nothing,** which he can serve them. Because of his need, he immediately goes to his neighbor. He explains to him that **"he has nothing"** and asks for bread. He continues to ask until he finally receives the bread. Now he has bread – bread of life – for himself and for his visitors. He has something for himself and is now in the position where he can share.

Now Jesus links this parable (problem: I have nothing) with the request for the Holy Spirit by saying: *"**Therefore** I say to you, ask, and it will be given you."* (Luke 11:9 NKJV) Then follows:

## Jesus' special Appeal: Therefore ask for the Holy Spirit

There is a particular Bible passage in which Jesus emphatically commands us to ask for the Holy Ghost. I know of no other passage where Jesus so lovingly urged us to take something to heart. These verses are found in His lesson on prayer in Luke 11. There He emphasized 10 times that we should ask for the Holy Spirit. Luke 11:9-13 NKJV:

*"So I say to you, **ask,** and it will be given to you; **seek,** and you will find; **knock,** and it will be opened to you. For everyone who **asks** receives, and he who **seeks** finds, and to him who knocks it will be opened. If a son **asks** for bread from any father among you, will he give him a stone? Or if he **asks** for a fish, will he give him a serpent instead of a fish? Or if he **asks** for an egg, will he offer him a scorpion? If you then, being evil, know how to give good gifts to your children, how much more will your heavenly Father give the Holy Spirit to those who **ask** Him!"*

In these few verses Jesus used the verb "ask" six times; then he replaced "ask" and emphasized it with "seek" two times – an action – and two more times with "knock" – also an action word.

Doesn't He clearly show us that we have to take action in order to be filled with the Holy Ghost? The last "ask" is used in the continuous tense in Greek. That means that we aren't to ask only once, but rather to ask continuously. Here Jesus doesn't only make asking a matter of urgency but also expects us to continually do it. Certainly He also wants to awaken our desire for the Holy Spirit with this heartfelt invitation. This urgent invitation shows us Jesus' conviction that we would be missing something crucial, if we don't continually ask for the outpouring of the Holy Ghost. He was clearly calling our attention to the fact that we absolutely need the Holy Spirit. In this way He wants us to continually receive the rich blessings of the Holy Ghost.

In *Christ's Object Lessons* it says: "God does not say, Ask once, and you shall receive. He bids us ask. Unwearyingly persist in prayer. The persistent asking brings the petitioner into a more earnest attitude, and gives him an increased desire to receive the things for which he asks".[1]

Jesus then gave three examples, which show behavior that is unimaginable even for sinful human fathers. He wanted to show us that it is even more unimaginable that our heavenly Father wouldn't give us the Holy Ghost when we ask. Jesus wants us to be sure that we will receive the Holy Ghost when we ask in the appropriate way. With this promise and other promises we can ask in faith and know that we have already received what we requested. (1 John 5:14-15; more information in chapter 5)

This special invitation shows us that according to Jesus something essential is missing, when we don't persistently ask for the Holy Ghost. He draws it to our attention that we absolutely need the Holy Ghost. He wants us to continually experience the rich blessings from the Holy Ghost.

This part of His lesson on prayer is a unique process. The Holy Spirit is God's greatest gift – the gift which brings all the other gifts with it. This was Jesus crowning gift to His disciples and clear proof of His love. I think we can understand that such a valuable gift wouldn't be

---

1    E.G. White, *Christ's Object Lessons* (1900), p. 145.3

pushed on someone. It is only given to those who express their desire for this gift and appreciate it.

He will be given to those who have surrendered their lives to Jesus; He will be given to those who live in continual commitment. (John 15: 4-5) Commitment is expressed by:

- A yearning for God (*"whoever thirsts"* John 7:37)
- Trust in God (*"he who believes in Me, as the Scripture has said"* John 7:38)
- Complete surrender as a result of trusting God (*"placing your whole life at God's disposal"* Rom. 12:1)
- Following God in everything (*"those who obey Him"* Acts 5:32)
- Give up their own way, go God's way and do this according to God's will (*"repent and be baptized"* Acts 2:38)
- Not to plan anything wrong (*"if I regard iniquity in my heart, the Lord will not hear"* Ps.66:18)
- Realize and admit to our great need (*"I have nothing"* Luke 11:6)
- Continually ask for the Holy Ghost (Luke 11:9-13)

Can't you clearly see in these expectations that God has for us, how valuable this gift is? When you think about all these prerequisites, then you will probably find deficiencies in yourself.

I have made it my habit to pray daily for a desire for the Holy Spirit in connection with John 7:37 NKJV: *"If anyone thirsts, let him come to Me and drink."* [2]

---

2   It is worthwhile to pray with promises. If you want to know more about this, please read chapter 4 of *Steps to Personal Revival*.

**We can pray:** "Lord Jesus, I completely say yes to all the prerequisites for receiving the Holy Ghost. I sincerely ask that you now – for today – fulfill them in me." Our wonderful God is even there for us in fulfilling the prerequisites.

## The Holy Spirit is the Source of a Fulfilled Life

According to Jesus why did He come to this earth? He said:

*"I have come that they may have life, and that they may have it more abundantly."* (John 10:10 NKJV)

Jesus wants us to experience this new life now and to continue it in a completely different dimension after His second coming as eternal life in God's kingdom.

He also shows us that the source of a fulfilled life is the Holy Ghost:

*"... 'If anyone thirsts, let him come to Me and drink. He who believes in Me, as the Scripture has said, out of his heart will flow rivers of living water.' But this He spoke concerning the Spirit ... ."* (John 7:37-39 NKJV)

"Rivers of living water" – isn't that a good comparison for a fulfilled life?

## During His life here on earth did Jesus give us a corresponding example?

We know that Mary conceived Jesus through the Holy Ghost. (Matt. 1:18). We know that after His baptism He prayed: *"And the Holy Spirit descended in bodily form like a dove upon Him ...."* (Luke 3:22) Under these circumstances was it necessary and important that He receive the Holy Spirit daily? I quote from E.G. White:

*"Morning by morning he communicated with his Father in heaven, receiving from him daily a fresh baptism of the Holy Spirit."* [3]

---

3   E.G. White, *Signs of the Times*, November 21, 1895, par. 3

There is a statement in *Acts of the Apostles*: "To the consecrated worker there is wonderful consolation in the knowledge that even Christ during His life on earth sought His Father daily for fresh supplies of needed grace ... ." [4]

Jesus indeed was an example to us in this. We have to ask ourselves: If Jesus daily needed a refreshing from the Holy Ghost, then how much more important is it for you and me?

The apostle Paul really understood Jesus' objective. In his letter to the church in Ephesus, Paul confirms in chapter 1:13 that they had been sealed by the Holy Ghost when they became believers. In chapter 3:16-17 he encourages them to be strong in the Spirit and in chapter 5:18 (NKJV) Paul, as an authorized apostle, calls the Ephesians and us to: "... *be filled with the Spirit*" or *"let yourselves be continuously and repeatedly filled again with the Spirit"* [5] We see that even if we received the Holy Spirit when we were born again, that we in general need a daily refreshing. It is important for the spiritual life and growth of a Christian to be daily filled with the Holy Ghost.

Our Sabbath School Study Guide says the following about Eph. 5:18: "What does it mean 'to be baptized' with the Holy Ghost? Jesus personally explained this with a synonym. A person is 'baptized' with the Holy Spirit (Acts 1:5) when the Holy Ghost 'has come upon' them (v. 8). To be baptized means to be fully immersed in something – usually water. This involves the whole person. Baptism with the Holy Spirit means to be completely under the influence of the Holy Ghost – to be completely 'filled' by Him. This isn't a one-time experience, but rather something that has to be continually repeated, as Paul illustrates in Eph. 5:18b with the tense of the Greek verb 'filled'." [6]

## Jesus' Farewell Words and the Holy Spirit

In Jesus' farewell words He conveyed joy and hope by telling them that the Holy Ghost would come in His place. Jesus tells something surprising to the disciples in John 16:7:

---

4   E.G. White, *The Acts of the Apostles*, (1911) p. 56.1
5   Johannes Mager, Auf den Spuren des Heiligen Geistes, (Lüneburg, 1999), Seite 101
6   Sabbath School Study Guide July 17, 2014

*"Nevertheless I tell you the truth. It is to your advantage that I go away; for if I do not go away, the Helper will not come to you; but if I depart, I will send Him to you."*

## A New Advantageous Solution

Jesus told the disciples something surprising: *"It is to your advantage that I go away."* This means that the new solution, that He is with us through the Holy Ghost, is more advantageous than Jesus being personally present. In this way He isn't limited, but rather He can be by each person, no matter where He currently is.

## A personal testimony from a teacher and one of her students:

When the booklet "Steps to Personal Revival" from H. Haubeil was handed out in my home church about a year ago, I read it through very quickly. Already while reading it I had more experiences with God than ever before – this fascinated and encouraged me.

In the booklet's appendix I found the following suggestion:
"Pedagogical research has shown that it is necessary to read or listen six to ten times to a vital topic till we have thoroughly understood it."
These encouraging words captivated my attention:
"Try it at least once. The result will convince you."

I wanted to experience that and already by the third reading it seized me and I felt a great love for our Redeemer, which I had yearned for my whole life. Within two months I had read it through six times and the result was worth it.

It was as if I could understand what it would be like when Jesus comes close to us and we can look into His pure, kind and loving eyes. From then on I didn't want to be without this joy in our Savior.

When I woke up in the morning I already yearned for my morning worship time in order to again experience fellowship with God and during the day I prayed quietly that the Holy Ghost would help me with my thoughts during conversations, my example, while teaching and communicating.

When a child craved attention and acted accordingly, God gave me strength and wisdom to deal with it.

Since then my work days are filled with the presence of the Creator. He helps me literally in my everyday life. Since then I pray in the morning and in between times for the outpouring of the Holy Ghost. It is as if you are closer to heaven and can already taste what it will be like there.

While reading the booklet the thought came to me that my students in the school should also share in this experience. I teach the 10-15 year-olds in our Adventist School Elijah in Vorarlberg, Austria. So I prayed for God to give me opportunities. Very soon afterwards I had one of my most wonderful experiences with how the Holy Ghost can work in young people's hearts.

## A 13 year-old Ruffian and the Holy Spirit

The experience started *a year before I read the booklet on the Holy Ghost*. A new student came to our school and within a few days our peaceful oasis was changed into a rough scuffle room. The boy was 13 years-old then – he was the biggest of all the children and correspondingly strong. Many things that had been learned during the school year and had brought wonderful fruit seemed to disappear in a moment.

Let him tell about it himself: "When I came to my present school, I had no idea what awaited me. On my second day of school I let myself get provoked, snapped and started a fight with one my classmates. I hit him even though he was considerably weaker than I was, berated him and never wanted to see him again.

Later I realized my mistake and apologized, just as I always had in the past. After that I had a conversation with the headmaster. In the next months a process started in me. It is astonishing that this process had only now started since I was a pastor's son. I started to spend more time with Jesus."

I thought that this young person would need extra special attention. He was aware of his failure, regretted it and tried again, but he didn't have long-lasting success in his own strength. At first, hardly a day would go by when he wasn't in a fight, but gradually it got better.

After 6 months he said he thought it was the prayers that had brought him closer to God. In the meantime he had started praying for strength in the morning. His fits of rage and fights became less frequent.

Eleven months had now gone by since he came to our school and we could see even more improvements. But his anger, his swearing outbursts and his fists weren't permanently under control.

It was only natural – he tried to win in his own strength and understanding, which worked sometimes and other times not at all. *Our prayers had made some achievement, but his mindset still wasn't right and the renewing power of the Spirit was missing.*

What good does it do, when a person sees their mistakes, tries to control their temper and in the next moment fails again? Just at the time when I realized that I was at my wits' end, I received the booklet mentioned above. It came at just the right time. Then I realized what we were missing. It was the power of the Holy Ghost. We hadn't even asked Him to help us!

Since I had been touched by the message of "Steps to Personal Revival" I got up my courage to ask the boy if he had ever prayed for the Holy Ghost. No – he never had. Then I tried to awaken his interest in the booklet. I didn't give it to him though. He should really want it. And very soon he did ask for the booklet.

Again in his own words: "In November 2012 my teacher gave me the booklet "Steps to Personal Revival". I eagerly started to read it. At that time I wasn't really acquainted with the work of the Holy Ghost."

Within the first day he had already devoured almost two chapters and then he asked me how many times I had read it. He immediately started to read the chapters again and wanted to do exactly what the booklet suggested: reading it 6-10 times.

Since then a lot has changed. From December 2012 on there weren't any more fist fights or scuffles – I could hardly believe it. The boys that he had beaten up every day became his friends and they get along harmoniously.

He has completely changed – he is polite and even obliging and peacefulness has taken over his aggressive nature. His classmates can confirm that God was at work. You can see the fruits every day. To God's glory I want to mention that the boy decided to get baptized in June 2013. If that wasn't the Holy Ghost. ...

I had always thought that I could manage a child and make it see reason. Patience, attention and lots of talks would do it, but it just didn't work long-term. God had to intervene and taught me that it is His Spirit, who makes the impossible possible.

Someday when this boy is in heaven, then I will know that God brought it about. When I was at the end of my wisdom and finally understood that I couldn't guide him, then God started to radically work on him. It encourages me to see that there are no hopeless cases for God. C.P.

*Prayer:* *Father in heaven, thank you for Jesus' urgent invitation to ask for the Holy Ghost. I am sorry for the losses I have experienced because of a lack of the Holy Ghost. I need divine assistance so that Jesus can become greater in me. I need His help in every area of my life. Thank you that the Holy Ghost can change my character and can make me fit for God's kingdom. I completely surrender myself to you with all that I am and have. Thank you for accepting me and giving me your blessings. Help me to grow in knowledge about the Holy Ghost. Amen.*

# CHAPTER 2

# WHAT IS THE CENTER OF OUR PROBLEMS?

*Is there a spiritual cause to our problems?*
*Is the cause a lack of the Holy Spirit?*

## CAUSES FOR THE DEFICIENCY

The Bible's answer is: *"Yet you do not have because you do not ask. You ask and do not receive, because you ask amiss* (according to the carnal mind, Rom. 8:5-7), *that you may spend it on your pleasures."* (James 4:2-3 NKJV)

Our Lord Jesus invited us lovingly and insistently to ask for the Holy Ghost (Luke 11:9-13). We understand that we should do this continually. In the third chapter we will look at this more closely.

> „*They talk about Christ and about the Holy Spirit, yet receive no benefit. They do not surrender the soul to be guided and controlled by the divine agencies."* [7]

We have been praying for a revival for some time. This is very valuable. E.G. White said: "It is this baptism of the Holy Spirit that the churches

---

7   Ellen G. White, *The Desire of Ages,* (1898), p. 672

need today." [8] "Why do we not hunger and thirst for the gift of the Spirit, since this is the means by which we are to receive power? Why do we not talk of it, pray for it, preach concerning it?" [9]

It is good that we pray for revival, but we shouldn't only pray for it, but rather – as Mark Finley says – it is **"as we put into practice the biblical elements of revival."** [10] May I invite you to take the steps to personal revival? For many this will lead to a more powerful and fulfilled life.

To start with, we want to analyze the problem. We want to do this thoroughly; otherwise there is the danger that we will consider a change neither necessary nor important. After that we want to look at God's solution, which offers us tremendous blessing and finally, how we can implement this and experience this.

Our lack of the Holy Spirit doesn't mean that everything we have done and are doing is in vain. There were and are many very good plans and programs. The Lord has surely blessed our human efforts. But how much greater the results and how much better the situation could be, when we would actually live or live more closely with the Holy Ghost – only God knows that.

It would have gone in this direction and would go in this direction in the future as Henry T. Blackaby expressed it:

"He (God) could do more in six months with a people that are devoted to Him, than we could do in sixty years without Him." [11]

It is the question of immediately going the right way under God's leadership and thus having much greater effectiveness (efficiency). That is the case when we are filled with the Holy Ghost.

Example: Someone holds a sermon. He is done speaking – maybe no one, a few, many or all accept the message. If many or all accepted the message and put it into practice, then this is great effectiveness. This is something the Holy Spirit gives.

---

8    E.G. White, *Manuscript Releases* Vol. 7  p. 267
9    E.G. White, *Testimonies for the Church* Vol. 8 (www.egwwritings.org), p. 22
10   Mark A. Finley, *Revive us again,* p. 25
11   Henry T. Blackaby, *Den Willen Gottes erkennen und tun (Experiencing God: Knowing and Doing the Will of God),* (Kassel, 2002), p. 31

# THREE GROUPS OF PEOPLE AND THEIR PERSONAL RELATIONSHIPS TO GOD

God's Word differentiates between three groups of people in respect to their personal relationships with God. Within each of these groups there are many different shades depending on the parental training, character, training of oneself, age, culture, education, etc. But even with all the differences there are **only three basic attitudes towards God:**

- ▸ No relationship – the Bible calls this the **natural** man.
- ▸ Full, real relationship – the Bible calls this person **spiritual.**
- ▸ Divided or feigned relationship – the Bible describes this as a person of the **flesh or carnal.**

The terms "natural", "spiritual" and "carnal" in God's Word are not evaluations in this case. They merely describe a person's personal relationship to God.

These three groups are described in 1 Corinthians 2:14-16 and 1 Corinthians 3:1-4. Right now we only want to touch lightly on the subject of the natural man. He lives in the world. A quick glance at the two groups within the church will help us realize where the problem is mainly hidden. The most important thing to realize is to which group you belong. Thus our examination also helps our self-diagnosis. We want to take a look at our own lives and not the lives of others.

*What are the criteria for designation in one group or the other?* We will determine that in all three groups the designation occurs according to their personal relationship with the Holy Ghost.

## The Natural Man

*"But the natural man **does not receive the things of the Spirit of God,** for they are foolishness to him; nor can he know them, because they are spiritually discerned."* (1 Corinthians 2:14 NKJV)

The natural man has absolutely no relationship with the Holy Ghost. He lives in the world and doesn't inquire about God at all or only rarely inquires about God.

## Spiritual and Carnal are in the Church

These two groups are mainly introduced in 1 Corinthians 2 and 3 as well as in Romans 8:1-17 and Galatians 4 and 6. We need to note that the **criterion for these two groups is their relationship to the Holy Ghost.** This is so, because God has stipulated that the Holy Ghost is our only connection to heaven. (The Desire of Ages, p. 322; Matt. 12:32) "The heart must be open to the Spirit's influence, or God's blessing cannot be received."[12]

## The Spiritual Church Member

Let's read 1 Corinthians 2:15-16:

*"But **he who is spiritual** judges all things, yet he himself is rightly judged by no one. For who has known the mind of the LORD that he may instruct Him?* (Isa. 40:13) **But we have the mind of Christ.**" (NKJV)

*"**The person with the Spirit** makes judgments about all things, but such a person is not subject to merely human judgments, for, Who has known the mind of the Lord so as to instruct him? **But we have the mind of Christ.**"* (NIV)

The spiritual person is the true Christian. He is called "spiritual", because he is filled with the Holy Ghost. Here too, the relationship with the Holy Ghost is the criteria for the designation as a spiritual person. He has a good and growing relationship with the Holy Spirit. Jesus is *"in the center of his life"*; we also say sometimes that Jesus is on our heart's throne. The spiritual person has committed himself essentially and completely to Jesus and as a general rule this is confirmed daily by surrendering himself to Jesus every morning with everything he is and has. In the Laodicea message he is called "hot", in the parable about the 10 virgins he is called "wise". Romans 8:1-17 and Galatians 5 say even more about him. He experiences life *"more abundantly"* (John 10:10) or as Paul expresses it: *"That you may be filled with all the fullness of God."* (Eph. 3:19; Col. 2:9)

---

12   E.G. White, *Leuchtende Spuren (Steps to Christ)* (Hamburg, 1959), p. 69

## The Carnal Church Member

A person can be a member for a short time or for many years and still be a carnal Christian. If to your surprise you find that you are a carnal Christian at the moment, then don't be upset about it, but rather be glad, because you have the possibility of changing it immediately. You will experience great joy through a life with the Holy Ghost. I am convinced that most carnal Christians are unknowingly in this condition and have a desire to experience more in their faith. Their ignorance if often not even their fault. Consider: you will experience great joy through a life with Christ in your heart through the Holy Ghost. (Jesus in John 15:11: *"and that your joy may be full."*) Through this change you will step by step experience life abundantly (Jesus in John 10:10 – more on this later) and you will have well-founded hope for eternal life.

> *Prayer: Father in heaven, please make me willing to ask myself this question. If I am a carnal Christian, then please help me to realize this right away. Make me willing to be willing for everything you want. Please lead me to a happy Christian life – to the promised life in abundance and to eternal life. Please renew my heart. Thank you for answering my prayer. Amen.*

Let's read what the apostle Paul had to say to carnal church members in 1 Corinthians 3:1-4 (NKJV): *"And I, brethren, could **not speak to you as to spiritual people** but as to carnal, as to babes in Christ. I fed you with milk and not with solid food; for until now you were not able to receive it, and even now you are still not able; for you are still carnal. For where there are envy, strife, and divisions among you, are you not carnal and behaving like mere men? For when one says, 'I am of Paul', and another, 'I am of Apollos', are you not carnal?"*

Can you clearly see here that the criteria for the designation into this group is the personal relationship with the Holy Ghost? In these few verses the apostle Paul mentions four times that they are carnal. What does carnal mean? It means: this person lives from the power of the flesh, that is the normal strength and abilities a person has. Furthermore, it means that he isn't filled with the Holy Ghost or isn't sufficiently filled with the Holy Ghost.

Some people think this group only consists of people, who live in blatant sin. But that is only one of the many shades within this group. I want to stress again that there are a lot of differences within each of these groups.

Paul addressed the carnal people as *"dear brothers"*. This shows that he was dealing with **church members.** Paul couldn't speak to them *"as to spiritual people"*. That means that: **They weren't filled with the Holy Ghost or weren't sufficiently filled with the Holy Ghost.** He had to speak to them *"as babes in Christ"*. This shows that they haven't grown in faith as they should have. A person can have great biblical knowledge and still not grow spiritually. Spiritual growth has to do with our complete dedication to Jesus and a constant life in the Holy Spirit.

Many carnal Christians feel dissatisfaction, disappointment, purposelessness or are under constant effort in their spiritual life.

Other carnal church members have gotten used to this condition or are satisfied with this condition. They might say: ›We are just sinners! We can't do anything about it!‹

Again other carnal Christians might be enthusiastic. They are glad that they know Biblical truth. Carnal church members can be very active and even have leading positions in the local church or even in the church administration. They may even do a lot for God.

> **Matt. 7:22-23 (NKJV):** *"Many will say to Me in that day, 'Lord, Lord, have we not prophesied in Your name, cast out demons in Your name, and done many wonders in Your name?' And then I will declare to them, ,I never knew you; depart from Me, you who practice lawlessness!'"*

Where did the problem lay? Jesus said that He didn't know them. They didn't have a real relationship with Christ, but rather only a feigned relationship. Either there hadn't been a real commitment or it hadn't been maintained. Jesus didn't live in their hearts through the Holy Ghost. Thus they had no personal relationship with Christ. "So there may be an apparent connection with Christ ..."[13] When isn't Christ in us? I read some serious words about this. Before I mention them, I want to point out that we can be free from the following things if we live a life with the Holy Ghost:

> "A spirit contrary to the spirit of Christ would deny Him, whatever the profession. Men may deny Christ by evilspeaking, by foolish talking, by words that are untruthful or unkind. They may deny Him by shunning life's burdens, by the pursuit of sinful pleasure. They may deny Him by conforming to the world, by uncourteous behavior, by the love of their own opinions, by justifying self, by cherishing doubt, borrowing trouble, and dwelling in darkness. **In all these ways they declare that Christ is not in them.**"[14]

This can quickly change by the grace of God. We will come back to this in the third and fifth section.

## Why is surrendering our lives and making a commitment to God important?

God's Word says: *"I beseech you therefore, brethren, by the mercies of God, that you present your bodies a living sacrifice, holy, acceptable to God, which is your reasonable service."* Rom.12:1 NKJV

"God desires to heal us, to set us free [from the tyranny of our ego and the bondage of sin]. But since this requires an entire transformation, a renewing of our whole nature, we must yield ourselves wholly to Him."[15] Our ego is offended, jealous, annoyed, resentful, etc. God wants to free us of these attitudes.

"He [God] invites us to give ourselves to Him, that He may work His will in us. It remains for us to choose whether we will be set free from the bondage of sin, to share the glorious liberty of the sons of God."[16]

---

13  E.G. White, *The Desire of Ages*, (1898), p. , S. 676
14  E.G. White, *The Desire of Ages*, (1898), p. S. 349
15  E.G. White, *Steps to Christ* (1892), p. 43.2
16  E.G. White, *Steps to Christ* (1892) p. 43.4

God answers our basic commitment with rebirth (John 3:1-21). After that it has to do with staying surrendered (John 15:1-17). We'll talk about this more in the third section.

> Morris Venden says about surrendering our lives to God:
> "There is no such thing as a partial surrender. It's no more possible to be partially surrendered than it is possible to be a little bit pregnant. Either you are or you aren't. There is no middle ground."[17]

> Ellen White said the following about daily surrender:
> "Only those who will become co-workers with Christ, only those who will say, Lord, all I have and all I am is Thine, will be acknowledged as sons and daughters of God."[18]

So a person can be in the church and still be lost. How tragic! (The parable about the 10 virgins and the message to the Laodicea church also illustrate this.)


### Why is carnal Christianity so difficult to identify?

Since a carnal person's life is filled with "religion", he often doesn't realize that he is missing something vital: an intimate and saving relationship with God. If Christ isn't allowed to govern our whole life, then He is standing in front of the door knocking (Rev. 3:20). And He says: If this doesn't change, then I will spit you out.

And something else plays a part. Through our strong doctrinal foundation, which is based on the Bible, we have strong convictions. (At the same time we still want to stay open to further insights.) We have the certainty that we believe the truth; that thrills us. We have a lot of good knowledge. We say the right things. That is what makes it so difficult to identify the carnal problem. Doesn't it play a role if I have ever really lived with the Holy Ghost? If not, then can I even notice the difference?

A pastor wrote: "I just received a call from a sister, who is taking part in our 40 day prayer time. (Particulars about the 40 day prayer time in chapter 5) She said that it has changed her life. **She had wondered her**

---

17   Morris Venden, *95 Theses on Righteousness by Faith* (Pacific Press, 1987), p. 63
18   E.G. White, *Desire of Ages*, p. 623

*I beseech you therefore, brethren, by the mercies of God, that you present your bodies a living sacrifice, holy, acceptable to God, which is your reasonable service.*

**whole life what was missing in her spiritual life and now she knew – the Holy Ghost.** I wish you could have heard her testimony. She said that she noticed for the first time in her life that she has a relationship with God. ... Others have also already noticed the change in her life."[19] We can see that a person can notice that something is missing, but doesn't know what. Many have a desire for more and don't know what it is or how to get it.

I am thankful that 1 Cor. 3:1-4 uses the word *"still"* three. *"For you are still carnal."* This shows us that it is possible for the carnal person to become spiritual. No one has to remain carnal. Since he is in the church he has a good chance to realize this and change it. We will talk later about how you can become spiritual.

Another aspect to consider is envy and strife or as the NIV says: *"There is jealousy and quarreling among you."* This behavior proves to Paul that the carnal church members are not living through God's Spirit, but rather acting carnally – just like other people. They can act just like natural people; albeit in religious packaging. Does this mean that tensions in the church stem mainly from carnal-minded church members? (See Jude v. 19) At the time of Jesus didn't the Pharisees and Sadducees rival with each other? This means that already back then there were tensions between the conservatives and the liberals/progressives. One group was very particular and the other took things loosely. But both were convinced that they had the correct Bible interpretation and attitude. But Jesus showed us that both groups were carnal, meaning not filled with

---

19   Email an H. Haubeil – received on February 15, 2012

the Holy Spirit. The same thing is possible today. Conservative Christians can also be carnal Christians.

Unfortunately, people today often look through the glasses of "conservative or liberal/progressive". The advantage is that the observer comes off well. However, with the biblical classification of "carnal or spiritual" we are challenged to take spiritual inventory. We should do this for our own good. Consider what God clearly tells us in Galatians 6:7-8 NKJV:

> "… whatever a man sows, that he will also reap. For he who sows to his flesh will of the flesh reap corruption, but he who sows to the Spirit will of the Spirit reap everlasting life."

The carnal person wants to follow Jesus and please Him, but he hasn't surrendered his whole life to Jesus or if he has then he has backslidden somehow. (Gal. 3:3; Rev. 2:4-5) That means that he, maybe unconsciously, wants to live according to God's will **and** his own wishes **simultaneously.** But that doesn't work. Ultimately he is carrying his own life in his hands. As the saying goes, there are two souls dwelling in his breast. Can God send the Holy Spirit in such a case? James 4:3 NKJV gives this answer: *"You ask and do not receive, because you ask amiss."* I have come to the conclusion that it means asking with a carnal attitude. Wouldn't an answer to such a request only boost the ego? Consequently, this church member is living through normal human powers and abilities. In Rev. 3:16 this is called »lukewarm« and in Matt. 25 "foolish".

## Why does Jesus call the carnal church members lukewarm?

Why is it that so many Christians are lacking an experience with the Holy Ghost? In order to answer this question, we will first have to take a look at the Laodicea phenomenon. Why did Jesus call the believers in the Laodicea church lukewarm? He gave us a clear indicator: *"Behold, I stand at the door and knock."* (Rev.3:20) Jesus wasn't the center of the lives of the believers, but rather outside. He was standing outside in front of the door. Why didn't He go in? Because He hadn't been invited. He doesn't force His way in, because He respects our free will decision.

Why do believers leave Jesus outside in front of the door? There are different causes and reasons for this. Some only move on a purely intellectual and cognitive plane in their spiritual lives, like the scribe

Nicodemus, and don't understand what the Christian life is all about. (Compare with John 3:1-10). For others the "price" of discipleship is too high, they have to give up too much, like the "rich young ruler". (Compare with Matt. 19:16-24). To follow Jesus it requires self-denial and the willingness to change his life (compare with Matt.16:24-25) and completely surrender himself to God (Rom.12:1). Leaving Jesus outside can be caused by pure negligence – insufficient time in personal fellowship with Jesus.

I repeat: the reason for the lukewarmness in Rev. 3:20 is: *"Behold, I stand at the door."* Jesus is not in the center of their lives, but rather outside or on the sidelines. So the lukewarmness relates to the personal relationship with Christ. In other areas the person concerned definitely doesn't have to be lukewarm.

An example: A man can invest a lot in his vocation and at the same time neglect his wife. He is committed to his job, but lukewarm in his marriage relationship. A person can even be a committed church member, a diligent church leader or pastor or president and still be lukewarm in his relationship with Christ. The person is so dedicated to accomplishing a lot of tasks, that he neglects his personal relationship with Christ. **This is the lukewarmness that Jesus wants removed.** It is tragic that a person can be so busy with God's work (in the church and mission work) that He neglects the Lord of the work.


## THE PARABLE OF THE TEN VIRGINS

What does Jesus' parable of the ten virgins show us in respect to the spiritual and carnal church members?

- ► All 10 were virgins
- ► All had pure biblical beliefs
- ► All had lamps
- ► All had the Bible
- ► All of them went to meet the bridegroom
- ► All of them looked forward to the 2nd coming
- ► All of them went to sleep
- ► All heard the call and woke up
- ► All prepared their lamps
- ► All the lamps were burning
- ► Half of them noticed that their lamps were going out

All of them prepared their lamps and **all of the lamps were burning; but burning lamps need oil. Energy was used.** After a short time five of them noticed that *their lamps were going out.* The lamps of the foolish virgins that only burned for a short time show us that they did have something from the Holy Spirit. But it wasn't enough. There was too little oil. **That was the only difference**.

When the five came asking to be let in, Jesus answered: *"I do not know you."* They were too late in attending to the oil, the Holy Ghost. The door remained closed.

Jesus' statement shows us that our personal relationship with Him has something to do with the Holy Ghost. Whoever doesn't let himself be led by the Holy Ghost won't be acknowledged by Jesus. In Rom. 8:8-9 it says: *"Those who are in the flesh cannot please God. ...if anyone does not have the Spirit of Christ, he is not His."*

Actually, we **only** have a real personal relationship with Jesus through the Holy Ghost. 1 John 3:24 says: *"And by this we know that He [Jesus] abides in us, by the Spirit whom He has given us."* This means that the assurance I have that I am filled with the Holy Ghost is at the same time the assurance that I am in Jesus and He is in me.

This is exactly the experience the sister had, who took part in the 40 day prayer time. Through the presence of the Holy Ghost in her life she experienced her relationship with God in a completely different way and others noticed the change in her life. A sister from southern Germany wrote the following after she had studied this booklet: "Together the book '40 Days – Prayers and Devotions to Prepare for the Second Coming' by Dennis Smith and this booklet have become a great and long-awaited blessing in my life. Just like many other church members and a sister from our church have experienced, something was always missing in our faith experience and now we have the privilege of experiencing how Jesus has entered our lives and has begun to change us. He is still working on us and step by step is drawing us closer to Him."[20]

A brother wrote the following: The booklet *Steps to Personal Revival* deeply touched me. The chapter on the ten virgins and especially on

---

20  Email from March 31, 2013

Romans 8:9b: *'Now if anyone does not have the Spirit of Christ, he is not His'* greatly shocked me. Suddenly, I wasn't sure if I had the Holy Ghost and if He was working in me, because I am painfully missing the corresponding "fruits" in my life. This Sabbath afternoon I finished reading the booklet and an infinitely deep sadness overwhelmed me. Then I read the prayer on page 108 and a deep desire rose in me to receive the Holy Ghost, that my heart would be changed and that God the Father would change me according to His will. ...Thank you for the booklet and the words, which deeply moved me." A.P

The greatest tragedy for the carnal Christian is that he won't receive eternal life if his condition doesn't change. Rom. 8:9b: *"Now if anyone does not have the Spirit of Christ, he is not His."*

Now to summarize: The main difference between the spiritual and the carnal church member has to do with the Holy Ghost. The spiritual Christian is filled with the Holy Spirit. The carnal Christian isn't or isn't sufficiently filled with the Holy Ghost.

Should you realize that you are a carnal Christian, then don't be angry. God is offering you a remedy: the Holy Ghost.

In some circles the Holy Ghost is overemphasized; on the other hand, in other circles He is neglected. May the Lord lead us on the path to the Biblical middle.


## COMPARISON: THE EARLY CHURCH AND THE CHURCH IN THE END TIMES

When we compare the early church with the present day church, we observe that the early church must have been predominantly made up of spiritual people. The book of Acts shows that this was the reason for their quick and positive development. They had no other aid. But they had the Holy Ghost. We have excellent aids in abundance. But we have a deficiency of the Holy Spirit.

Remember what A. W. Tozer said: "If the Holy Ghost were taken away from our church today, 95% of what we do would continue and no one would notice the difference. If the Holy Ghost had withdrawn from the early church, then 95% (this means almost everything) of what they were doing would have stopped and everyone would have noticed the difference." [21]

## Have we learned to get along without the Holy Ghost? Does the church today consist primarily of carnal Christians?

As a consequence, are we often powerless and to a large extent have no victories? Does a carnal attitude have something to do with the fact that we only have weak church growth in many places? Do many of the serious problems in many areas come from carnal attitudes? We will notice more and more that our personal and mutual central problem is the lack of the Holy Spirit. In the personal area we can quickly change this with God's help.

The following statement made for ministers naturally applies to everyone.

Johannes Mager says: "Paul differentiates between spiritual and carnal Christians, between those who are filled with the Holy Spirit and those who have no room for the Holy Spirit in their lives: baptized with the Holy Ghost, but not filled with the Holy Ghost.

For a minister this means that: I can have sound theological training, be well-versed in the basic biblical languages and skillfully practice exegesis; I can have received the great biblical truths intellectually and understood them and be well-versed in the dogmatic theology of different centuries; I can have a sound grasp of homiletics and preach relevant and realistic sermons – and despite all my knowledge and talents not be filled with the Holy Ghost. Books, education, good technical equipment, even charisma form a substitute for the missing Spirit-filled life.

Preaching, praying publically, organizing church life, preparing evangelistic programs, giving pastoral counseling – these all can be learned and also put into practice without the Holy Ghost. Ellen G. White described this dangerous possibility as follows: "The reason why there is so

---

21  Dr. S. Joseph Kidder, *Anleitung zum geistlichen Leben* (Andrews University), PPP Folie 2

little of the Spirit of God manifested is that ministers learn to do without it." (E.G. White, Testimonies for the Church, Volume 1, (1868), p. 383.1)

Johannes Mager was a pastor, evangelist and a professor of systematic theology for many years. He worked last as secretary of the ministerial department of the Euro-African Division (now: Inter-European Division) in Bern, Switzerland. He is now retired and lives in Friedensau, Germany. [22]

> *To summarize: Being carnal means living by normal human powers and abilities without the Holy Ghost or an insufficient quantity of the Holy Spirit.*

## THE MAIN OBSTACLE IN CARNAL CHRISTIANITY

The great ethics of the Bible – loving your enemy, forgiving people for everything, overcoming sin, etc. – can only be achieved by the power of the Holy Spirit, not with human effort. This shows us that the main problem in carnal Christianity is that it is a life solely in human strength. We can't do God's will alone in our own strength. Let's read a few Bible verses to this topic:

**Isaiah 64:6 NKJV:** *"And all **our** righteousnesses are like filthy rags."*

**Jer. 13:23 NKJV:** *"Can the Ethiopian change his skin or the leopard its spots? Then may you also do good who are accustomed to do evil."*

**Ezekiel 36:26-27 NKJV:** *"I will give you a new heart and put a new spirit within you.... I will put My Spirit within you and cause you to walk in My statutes, and you will keep My judgments and do them."*

**Rom. 8:7 NKJV:** *"Because the carnal mind is enmity against God: for it is not subject to the law of God, **nor indeed can be.**"* And NIV: *"The mind governed by the flesh is hostile to God; it does not submit to God's law, **nor can it do so.**"*

---

22  Johannes Mager, *Auf den Spuren des Heiligen Geistes (Following the Steps of the Holy Ghost)*, (Lüneberg, 1999), pages 102-103.

Ellen White said very clearly and accurately:

"He who is trying to reach heaven by his own works in keeping the law, is attempting an impossibility. Man cannot be saved without obedience, **but his works should not be of himself; Christ should work in him to will and to do of his good pleasure."** [23]

I think these references show sufficiently that we are not capable of doing God's will without the Holy Ghost. Our main concern is that we always need to make a decision for God's will and that God gives us the strength to implement it. This understanding of the doctrine of righteousness by faith is extremely important and liberating. However, we can't discuss it in detail here.

## WHAT COULD HAPPEN, WHEN SOMEONE TRIES TO DO SOMETHING THAT EXCEEDS THEIR STRENGTH?

What happens when I often realize: I can't do it! Now I've failed again! I think that to some degree we experience disappointment.

I think this problem is much more prominent in the younger generation rather than the older one. Older people are used to a stronger sense of duty, obedience in the family, school and business. Thus they aren't as easily annoyed by a disappointment as younger people are. But the problem is equally present in young and old. Only a younger person notices it more distinctly. Traveling the path of faith in their own strength is the foremost problem of every carnal Christian, whether he knows it or not.

How do we try to solve this problem? One person may pray more intensely for God's help and decide to try harder. Another person may think that we shouldn't be so narrow-minded. Now he starts to take things more casually and feels freer. Still another completely abandons his faith and may even feel better. The only problem is that these apparent solutions are false solutions, because the consequences will come sooner or later. The correct way is to take God's laws seriously, because they were given in love and are for our own good. However, we need God's strength for this. The right way is to live in the power of the Holy Spirit with increasing joy, motivation, strength, fruitfulness and victory.

---

23  E.G. White, *Review and Herald,* July 1, 1890

## THE CENTRAL PROBLEM

I think we have recognized that this mostly has to do with carnal Christianity. Isn't it becoming clearer and clearer why Jesus doesn't want any lukewarm followers? They don't have life in abundance like God wants to give us and they are a bad example even though most of them don't even know it. The problem is much more serious than we think. "Half-hearted Christians are worse than infidels; for their deceptive words and noncommittal position lead many astray." [24]

In the book *Christ our Righteousness* by Arthur G. Daniells we read the following:
"But formalism is something extremely deceptive and destructive. It is the hidden, unexpected cliff, which the church has threatened to shatter on many times throughout the centuries. Paul warned us that this *'form of Godliness'* (2 Tim. 3:5) without God's power [without being filled by the Holy Ghost] would be one of the dangers of the last days and admonishes us not to be taken in by this comfortable, self-deceiving attitude."[25]

## Possible Factors leading to Carnal Christianity

The following factors or reasons are things which can lead to carnal Christianity:

1. **Ignorance** – We haven't devoted ourselves enough to the topic of »life with the Holy Ghost« or we haven't found the key for putting it into practice.

2. **Unbelief or Small of Faith** – Being filled with the Holy Ghost has the prerequisite of completely surrendering our lives to Jesus Christ. This too could happen because of ignorance, or maybe because we are afraid that the Lord will lead us differently than what we want. This means that we don't trust God's love and wisdom enough.

---

24  EGW Letter 44, 1903, quoted in *Adv. Bible Commentary*, Vol.7, p.963 on Rev. 3: 15-16
25  Arthur G. Daniells, *Christ our Righteousness*, p. 20

3. **Erroneous Notions** – A person can think they are filled with the Holy Spirit, even though they aren't in reality or not sufficiently. This seems to be the most frequent problem.

4. **Being too Busy** – People are so overburdened that they think they don't have any or enough time to maintain a relationship with Christ. Or they take the time, but don't make any progress in connecting with God.

5. **Hidden Sins,** perhaps missing reparation – this is like a short-circuit, meaning there is no connection with God's power.

6. **Act mostly according to their feelings.** God's word says: *"The righteous live by faith".* Do I make decisions by trusting God or according to my feelings? This statement from Roger Morneau really impressed me: *"The spirits would encourage people to listen to their feelings instead of the word of Christ and His prophets. In no surer way could the spirits obtain control of people's lives without the individuals realizing what was happening."*[26]

## Why should I ask for the Holy Ghost, even though I am already filled with the Holy Ghost?

On one hand, the Holy Ghost was given to us in order to stay in us. On the other hand, we should continually ask by faith for the Holy Ghost. How do we solve this apparent contradiction?

On one hand:
Jesus said in John 14:17 NKJV: *"For He [the Holy Ghost] dwells with you and will be in you."* Acts 2:38 NKJV says: *"Repent, and let every one of you be baptized ... and you shall receive the gift of the Holy Spirit."*
On the other hand:
When Jesus taught about prayer, He said in Luke 11: 9-13 (NKJV): *"... ask, and it will be given to you; ...how much more will your heavenly Father give the Holy Spirit to those who ask Him!"* Ephesians 5:18 says: *"... be filled with the Spirit."* In both cases in the original Greek text, it is a continual request.

---

26   Roger Morneau, A Trip into the Supernatural, Review and Herald 1982, p. 43

Solution:

E.G. White says: "Yet the operations of the Spirit are always in harmony with the written word. As in the natural, so in the spiritual world. The natural life is preserved moment by moment by divine power; yet it is not sustained by a direct miracle, but through the use of blessings placed within our reach. So the spiritual life is sustained by the use of those means that Providence has supplied. If the follower of Christ would grow up 'unto a perfect man, unto the measure of the stature of the fullness of Christ' (Ephesians 4:13), he must eat of the bread of life and drink of the water of salvation. He must watch and pray and work, in all things giving heed to the instructions of God in His word." [27]

We received life at our birth. In order to sustain this life we have to eat, drink, exercise, etc. It is exactly the same in our spiritual life. We have the Holy Ghost through our baptism by water and the Spirit (born again) so that this spiritual life remains in us our whole life. In order to sustain this spiritual life it is necessary to use the spiritual means that God provided: the Holy Ghost, God's Word, prayer, our testimony, etc.

Jesus said in John 15:4: *"Abide in me, and I in you."* E.G. White says concerning this: "Abiding in Christ means a constant receiving of His Spirit, a life of unreserved surrender to His service." [28]

That is why we need to daily ask for the Holy Ghost by faith and surrender ourselves to the Lord every morning with everything we have and are.

## WHERE DO I STAND?

Now the most important thing is to discern which group I am in. Where do I stand?

When my dear mother was 20 she answered a man's question by saying that she wasn't interested in faith. He then replied: And if you died in the night? This comment hit her hard. But it had a very positive effect. It led her to make a decision for Jesus and His church. Maybe this question will help you too:

---

27  E.G. White, *The Acts of the Apostles,* (1911), p. 284.2
28  E.G. White, *The Desire of Ages,* (1898), p. 676.2

*Suppose ... you died today...! (heart attack? accident?)*
*Do you have the assurance of eternal life with Jesus Christ?*
*Don't remain uncertain.*

## Something Alarming

I am very alarmed as I have begun to understand the great magnitude of this problem. I have thought and prayed about if I should really add this paragraph. I am taking the chance since it is a matter of happiness in life now and eternal life and it also especially has an influence on marriage and family as well as the church and occupation. I don't know who it applies to. But I want to be of help to the persons concerned, since I have been helped as well. It is crucial that everyone that is carnal realizes this; otherwise he can't change with God's help. God in His love wants to richly bless us through an intimate relationship with Jesus Christ through the Holy Ghost. As a result great loss can be avoided and immeasurable blessing can be experienced. And the wonderful thing is that we can quickly remedy the situation with God's help. (In more detail in chapters 3 and 5)

The problem of carnal Christianity is described in the Bible in different ways. Individual groups and the people in the groups can have very different focal points, but the central problem is the same. The different descriptions are:

- **"in the flesh or carnal"** – Rom.8:1-17; 1 Cor. 3:1-4, Gal. 5:16-21 and other texts
- **"foolish"** – the parable of the ten virgins Matt. 25:1-13
  "The state of the Church represented by the foolish virgins, is also spoken of as the Laodicean state." [29]
- **"lukewarm"** – the letter to Laodicea Rev. 3:14-21
  *"I could wish you were cold or hot."* (Rev. 3:15) Isn't it amazing? Jesus prefers cold to lukewarm. What is His reason for this? "Halfhearted Christians are worse than infidels; for their deceptive words and noncommittal position lead many astray. The infidel shows his colors. The lukewarm Christian deceives both parties. He is neither a good worldling nor a good Christian. Satan uses him to do a work that no one else can do." [30]

---

29  E.G. White, *Review and Herald,* Aug. 19, 1890
30  E.G. White, Letter 44, 1903, quoted in the *Seventh Day Adventist Bible Commentary,* Vol.7, p. 963 on Rev. 3: 15.16

- **not "born again"** or hasn't remained in this condition – John 3:1-21
  "The new birth is a rare experience in this age of the world. This is the reason why there are so many perplexities in the churches. Many, so many, who assume the name of Christ are unsanctified and unholy. They have been baptized, but they were buried alive. Self did not die, and therefore they did not rise to newness of life in Christ." [31]
- **a form of godliness** – *"Having a form of godliness but denying its power."* 2 Tim. 3:5 Arthur G. Daniells says the following about this:
  "... But formalism is something extremely deceptive and destructive. It is the hidden, unexpected cliff, which the church has threatened to shatter on many times throughout the centuries. Paul warned us that this 'form of Godliness' (2 Tim. 3:5) without God's power [without being filled by the Holy Ghost] would be one of the dangers of the last days and admonishes us not to be taken in by this comfortable, self-deceiving attitude." [32]

And there are also some shocking statements in Ellen White's writings:

- **Very, very few**
  "In my dream a sentinel stood at the door of an important building, and asked every one who came for entrance, 'Have ye received the Holy Ghost?' A measuring-line was in his hand, and only very, very few were admitted into the building." [33]
- **Not one in twenty are ready**
  "It is a solemn statement that I make to the church, that not one in twenty whose names are registered upon the church books are prepared to close their earthly history, and would be as verily without God and without hope in the world as the common sinner." [34]

---

31  E.G. White, MS 148, 1897, quoted in the *Seventh Day Adventist Bible Commentary* Vol.6, p. 1075 Many buried alive
32  A. G. Daniells, *Christ our Righteousness*, p. 20
33  E.G. White, *Selected Messages*, Vol. 1 (1958), p. 109.2
34  E.G. White, *Christian Service* (1925), p. 41.1

- **Why are we so sleepy?**

  "Why are the soldiers of Christ so sleepy and indifferent? Because they have so little real connection with Christ; because they are so destitute of His Spirit." [35]

- **A great danger**

  "I will not here dwell upon the shortness and uncertainty of life; but there is a terrible danger – a danger not sufficiently understood – in delaying to yield to the pleading voice of God's Holy Spirit, in choosing to live in sin; for such this delay really is." [36] What is at the core of sin? *"Because they do not believe in Me."* (John 16:9) The sign that we really believe and trust Jesus is that we completely surrender ourselves to Him. It has to do with our complete surrender; our willingness to follow Him in everything.

I want to say it again: I took the chance of adding this very serious paragraph, because it has to do with our personal happiness in life and our eternal life, and also with our influence especially on our marriages, families and churches.

## Questions and more Questions

The crucial question is if you are filled with the Holy Ghost or not. But when is a person filled with the Holy Ghost? What are the necessary prerequisites? What are the positive results of a life with the Holy Spirit? What happens, when you erroneously think you are filled with the Holy Ghost?

## Be Thankful for the Signals

Thank the Lord that we are devoting ourselves more to the topic of revival. I think that our great and marvelous God has important reasons for presently giving us impulses by the Holy Spirit for a revival. Could these be the reasons?

---

35  E.G. White, *The Great Controversy* (1911), p. 507.3
36  E.G. White, *Selected Messages*, Vol. 1 (1958), p. 109.2

- He wants to relieve our deficiency and lead us out of our Laodicea-like state.
- He wants to prepare us for the soon second coming of Jesus and the special time just before it happens.
- He wants to bring about the great closing revival (Rev. 18:1-2) in the world through those, *"who keep the commandments of God and have the testimony of Jesus Christ"* (Rev. 12:17 NKJV) and have *"the faith of Jesus"*. (Rev. 12:17 NKJV)

Let us also thank God that every carnal Christian can quickly become a spiritual Christian. And that everyone who lives in the Holy Ghost can grow to the fullness of Christ. This is now our next job. Now for one more experience at the end of this chapter.

## New Motivation and Inner Joy

"A sister in the church gave me the booklet *'Steps to Personal Revival'.* I was overwhelmed by the contents of the booklet. I had long been searching for something like this and had finally found it. I then started to organize my spiritual life and only then did I realize that I had to do something: I surrendered myself completely to Jesus. From then on the Lord woke me up very early and gave me time for my personal devotions. Every day I studied a chapter in the 40-Days book. I noticed clearly that my relationship with Jesus grew greater. It became deeper and more intimate. The Holy Ghost was working on me. After the 40-Days book, I studied book two of the 40-Days. Since then I gave studied each of these books four times. I can't do anything but daily ask for fellowship with God. The results are awesome, because my new motivation and inner joy can't remain unnoticed. During this time I have had the privilege of having a lot of experiences with God. I also looked for opportunities to share my experience. A close relationship with Jesus makes many things become unimportant and needless cares are solved. I hope and pray that many people will have this experience that I have been privileged to have." H. S.

# CHAPTER 3

# OUR PROBLEMS ARE THEY SOLVABLE – HOW?

*How can we grow to be happy and strong Christians?*
*How can the Holy Spirit fill our lives?*

> Jesus said:
> "Abide in Me, and I in you." (John 15:4)
> "Abiding in Christ means a constant receiving of His Spirit, a life of unreserved surrender to His service." [37]

This two-part divine solution for our central problem is at the same time the way to a happy Christian life. Why? Jesus commented on these words: *"These things I have spoken to you, that My Joy may remain in you, and that your joy may be full."* ( John 15:11 NKJV) Through these two steps (continually receiving the Holy Spirit and complete surrender) Christ lives in us and it is the way to perfect happiness. Col. 1:17 speaks about the riches of the glory: Christ in you. Isn't it remarkable that Jesus

---

[37] E.G. White, *The Desire of Ages* (1898), p. 676.2

embedded this parable of the vine in the promise for the Holy Ghost in John 14 and the work of the Holy Ghost in John 16?

> *The crucial point is that we (as a rule) daily surrender ourselves to God including everything we are and have and that we also daily ask and receive by faith the outpouring of the Holy Ghost.*

## WHY IS IT NECESSARY TO SURRENDER OURSELVES TO JESUS DAILY?

Jesus said in Luke 9:23: *"If anyone desires to come after Me, let him deny himself, and take up his cross **daily**, and follow Me."*

Jesus said that discipleship is a daily matter. To deny oneself means giving Jesus the control over my life. Carrying a cross doesn't mean that we will have difficulties every day. Here is means: to daily deny our egos and to submit gladly and willingly to Jesus – just as Paul said about himself: "I die daily." When someone carried a cross in Jesus' day, then he had been sentenced to death and was going to the place of execution. So it also has to do with accepting difficulties, which arise from following Jesus.

We received our physical life at birth. In order to maintain our life, strength and health we normally eat every day. We received our spiritual life when we were born again. In order to keep our spiritual life strong and healthy it is also necessary to take care of the inner person **daily.** If this doesn't take place in our physical life as well as in our spiritual life, then we will become weak, sick or even die. We can neither eat meals ahead as reserve meals nor can we stockpile the Holy Ghost.

In the book *The Acts of the Apostles* there is a valuable advice on this: "As in the natural, so in the spiritual world. The natural life is preserved moment by moment by divine power; yet it is not sustained by a direct miracle, but through the use of blessings placed within our reach. So the spiritual life is sustained by the use of those means that Providence has supplied."[38]

---

38 E.G. White, *The Acts of the Apostles,* (1911), p. 284.2

This comment in the book *The Desire of Ages* really impressed me: " We are to follow Christ day by day. God does not bestow help for tomorrow." [39]

Ellen White said:

"To follow Jesus requires wholehearted conversion at the start, and a repetition of this conversion **every day.**" [40] "However complete may have been our consecration at conversion, it will avail us nothing unless it be renewed **daily** ...." [41] "Consecrate yourself to God in the morning; make this your very first work. Let your prayer be, "Take me, O Lord, as wholly Thine. I lay all may plans at Thy feet. Use me today in Thy service. Abide with me, and let all my work be wrought in Thee." This is a daily matter. Each morning consecrate yourself to God for that day. Surrender all your plans to Him, to be carried out or given up as His providence shall indicate. Thus day by day you say be giving your life into the hands of God, and thus your life will be molded more and more after the life of Christ." [42]

Morris Venden said:

"If you haven't discovered the necessity of daily conversion, it can be a major breakthrough in your life. Thoughts From The Mount of Blessing, page 101, makes this promise: 'If you will seek the Lord and be converted every day ... all your murmurings will be stilled, all your difficulties will be moved, all the perplexing problems that now confront you will be solved.'" [43]

Remaining with Jesus through a daily renewal of our surrender is just as important as it was when we first came to Him.

Morris Venden says further: "The abiding daily relationship with God leads to abiding surrender, moment-by-moment dependence on Him." [44]

---

**39** E.G. White, *The Desire of Ages* (1898), p. 313.4

**40** Editor Francis D. Nichol, *Adventist Bible Commentary Vol. 1* (Review and Herald, 1976), p. 1113

**41** E.G. White, Review and Herald, Jan. 6, 1885

**42** E.G. White, Steps to Christ (1892), p. 70.1

**43** Morris Venden, *95 Theses on Righteousness by Faith* (Pacific Press, 1987), p. 96

**44** Morris Venden, 95 *Theses on Righteousness by Faith* (Pacific Press, 1987), p. 233

We may be certain that: when we consciously surrender ourselves to Jesus every morning, then we are doing what He wishes us to do, because He said: *"Come to me..."* (Matt. 11:28 NKJV) and: *"... the one who comes to Me I will by no means cast out."* (John 6:37 NKJV)

"The Lord is willing to do great things for us. We shall not gain the victory through numbers, but through the full surrender of the soul to Jesus. We are to go forward in His strength, trusting in the mighty God of Israel ..." [45]

The great influence that God can exert through us when we completely surrender ourselves to Him is described by John Wesley as follows: "God can do more with one man, who has committed himself 100% to God, than He can with a whole army of men, who have only committed themselves 99% to God." [46]

Ellen White wrote:

"Only those who will become co-workers with Christ, only those who will say, Lord, all I have and all I am is Thine, will be acknowledged as sons and daughters of God. "[47] "All who consecrate soul, body, and spirit to God will be constantly receiving a new endowment of physical and mental power... The Holy Spirit puts forth its highest energies to work in heart and mind. The grace of God enlarges and multiplies their faculties, and every perfection of the divine nature comes to their assistance in the work of saving souls ... And in their human weakness they are enabled to do the deeds of Omnipotence." [48]

So much to the topic of daily "consecration" or "commitment" or "surrendering your life" or "conversion".

---

45  E.G. White, *Sons and Daughters of God*, p. 279
46  Dr. S. Joseph Kidder, Anleitung zum geistlichen Leben (Andrews University), PPP slide 14
47  E.G. White, *The Desire of Ages* (1898), p. 523.1
48  E.G. White, *The Desire of Ages* (1898), p. 827.3

## Why should a person daily ask for a new baptism of the Holy Spirit?

The request to be filled with the Holy Ghost is a request to Jesus to stay by me. Because He lives in me through the Holy Ghost. But why daily?

E.G. White said in *The Acts of the Apostles:* "To the consecrated worker there is wonderful consolation in the knowledge that even Christ during His life on earth sought His Father **daily for fresh supplies of needed grace** ... His own example is an assurance that earnest, persevering supplication to God in faith – faith that leads to entire dependence upon God, and unreserved consecration to His work – will avail to bring men the Holy Spirit's aid in the battle against sin." [49]

If this was a daily necessity for Jesus, then how much more important it is for us.

In 2 Cor. 4:16 NKJV there is an important statement:
*"... yet the inward man is being **renewed day by day."**

Our inward man needs daily care. In what way does this daily renewal take place? According to Eph. 3:16-17, 19 NKJV it happens through the Holy Ghost: *"That He would grant you, according to the riches of His glory,* ***to be strengthened with might through His Spirit in the inner man,*** *that Christ may dwell in your hearts through faith; that you, being rooted and grounded in love, ... that you may be filled with all the fullness of God."*

As a consequence:
- As a rule it is necessary to pray daily for a renewal of the Holy Spirit.
- As a result Christ lives in us.
- He gives us power according to the riches of His glory for our inner man. The power of God is a supernatural power.
- Thus God's love is put into our hearts.
- And it is the way to a life "with all the fullness of God". (see John 10:10; Col. 2:10)

---

49  E.G. White, *Acts of the Apostles*, (1911), p. 56.1

Another important text is found in Eph. 5:18 NKJV: "... *be filled with the Spirit.*" Take note that this is more than just advice. It is a divine command. Our God expects us to want to live with the Holy Ghost. The Greek experts say that this text says more precisely – and I am quoting Johannes Mager: "Let yourselves be consistently and continually filled anew with the Ghost." [50]

Our lesson study guide says: "Baptism with the Holy Spirit means to be completely under the influence of the Holy Ghost - to be completely `filled´ by Him. This isn't a one-time experience, but rather something that has to be continually repeated, as Paul illustrates in Eph. 5:18 with the tense of the Greek verb 'filled'." [51]

The apostle Paul wrote this in Ephesians chapter 5, even though he wrote the following in chapter 1:13: "... in whom also, having believed, you were sealed with the Holy Spirit of promise." The Ephesians had evidently already received the Holy Ghost. Nevertheless, it was necessary for them to be: "strengthened with might through His Spirit" and to "be filled with the Spirit" and "let yourselves be consistently and continually filled with the Ghost anew". In chapter 4:30 he warns us not to grieve or to insult the Holy Ghost.

Ellen White said:

"For the **daily** baptism of the Spirit every worker should offer his petition to God." [52]

"In order that we may have the righteousness of Christ, we need daily to be transformed by the influence of the Spirit, to be a partaker of the divine nature. It is the work of the Holy Spirit to elevate the taste, to sanctify the heart, to ennoble the whole man". [53]

---

50  Editor Werner E. Lange, *Unser größtes Bedürfnis* (Lüneburg, 2011), p. 42
51  Sabbath School Study Guide July 17, 2014
52  E.G. White, *The Acts of the Apostles* (1911), p. 50.2
53  E.G. White, *Selected Messages 1*, (1958), p. 374.1

The Lord said in another place through her: "Those who have been impressed by the Holy Scriptures as the voice of God, and desire to follow its teachings, are to be **daily** learning, **daily** receiving **spiritual fervor and power,** which have been provided for every true believer in the gift of the Holy Spirit." [54]

In addition she said: "We are to follow Christ day by day. God does not bestow help for tomorrow." [55]

And in another place: "A connection with the divine agency every moment is essential to our progress. We may have had a measure of the Spirit of God, but by prayer and faith we are **continually to seek more of the Spirit."** [56]

I also found this amazing quote: **"You need a daily baptism of the love** that in the days of the apostles made them all of one accord." [57]

Rom. 5:5 shows us that God's love is poured into our hearts by the Holy Ghost. We find the same thing in Eph. 3:17. The daily baptism with the Holy Ghost (being filled with the Holy Ghost) causes at the same time a daily baptism with love (being filled with God's agape love). In addition, it says in Gal. 5:16 that as a result the power of sin is broken.


## THE IMPORTANCE OF PERSONAL WORSHIP

What importance does personal worship have, if it is so important that I daily surrender to Jesus and ask to be filled with the Holy Ghost?

Daily worship and the observance of the Sabbath are the foundation for a spiritual life.

We have already read Bible verses and diverse quotes. They show us that the inner person is renewed day by day. **This casts a clear light on the great importance of our daily personal worship.**

The whole foundation for the worship service in the tabernacle was the morning and evening burnt offerings. On Sabbath there was an additional Sabbath burnt offering (Num. 28:4,10). What importance did the burnt offering have?

---

54  E.G. White, *The Signs of the Times March 8,* 1910, par. 1
55  E.G. White, *The Desire of Ages* (1898), p. 313.4
56  E.G. White, *The Review and Herald,* March 2, 1897, par. 5
57  E.G. White, *Testimonies to the Church* (1904), vol. 8, p. 191

"The burnt offering represented the complete surrender of the sinner to the Lord. Here the person kept nothing for themselves, but rather everything belonged to God."[58]

"The hours appointed for the morning and the evening sacrifice were regarded as sacred, and they came to be observed as the set time for worship throughout the Jewish nation ... In this custom Christians have an example for morning and evening prayer. While God condemns a mere round of ceremonies, without the spirit of worship, He looks with great pleasure upon those who love Him, bowing morning and evening to seek pardon for sins committed and to present their requests for needed blessings."[59]

Do you notice that daily worship is connected with the Sabbath as a basis for our spiritual lives? In addition, does it make it clear that it has to do with a daily surrender to Jesus Christ, who is invited through the Holly Ghost to live in us?

Have you made the most important spiritual principle your own: To give God priority over everything every day? Jesus said in the Sermon on the Mount:

*"But seek first the kingdom of God and His righteousness, and all these things shall be added to you."* Matt.6:33 NKJV

The kingdom of God is when you have Christ in your heart now. This is why we need daily surrender and to daily ask for the Holy Spirit during our worship time. The decisive moment will be when we stand before God: Did we have the saving personal relationship with Christ and did we stay in Him? (see John 15:1-17) Don't you long for more – for greater fulfillment in your faith?

Whoever spends little or no quiet time with God or only has an inadequate worship time will probably only be strengthened by their worship once or twice a week. That is similar to someone only eating once a week. To make a comparison: Wouldn't it be absurd to only want to nourish yourself once a week? Doesn't this mean that a Christian without worship is carnal?

---

58  Fritz Rienecker, *Lexikon zur Bibel* (Wuppertal, 1964), p. 1017
59  E.G. White, *Patriarchs and Prophets* (1890) p. 353.3

*In order that we may have the righteousness of Christ, we need daily to be transformed by the influence of the Spirit, to be a partaker of the divine nature.*

This also means that if he stays in this condition then he isn't saved. When we are carnal Christians worship can be just an obligation. When we are spiritual then worship will become more and more a necessity.

Years ago I read a booklet by Jim Vaus: *I was a Gangster*. He was a criminal, who became converted. He wholeheartedly confessed his sins – for example perjury, theft, etc. He experienced tremendous divine intervention. This impressed me. I said to myself: I am doing fine in almost every way, but I don't have experiences like that. Then I prayed to the Lord: "Father in heaven, I also want to confess all my known sins and all the sins that you will yet show me. In addition, I will get up an hour earlier to pray and read the Bible. Then I want to see if you will also intervene in my life."

Praise God! He intervened in my life. Since then, especially my morning worship in connection with the Sabbath, has become the basis for my life with God.

> *Through daily surrender and through being daily filled with the Holy Ghost our lives will be beneficially changed. This happens during our personal worship time.*

### WORSHIP IN SPIRIT AND IN TRUTH

Let's think about the objective of worship. In God's last message to humanity it has to do with worshipping the creator in contrast to worshipping the beast. (Rev. 14:6-12) The outward sign of worship is the Sabbath (worshipping the creator). The inner attitude of worship is shown in John 4:23-24: *"But the hour is coming, and now is, when **the true worshipers will worship the Father in spirit and truth;** for the Father is seeking such to worship Him. God is Spirit, and those who worship Him **must** worship in spirit and truth."*

**To worship in spirit** certainly means to worship consciously, but also to be filled with the Holy Ghost. **To worship in truth** means living in complete surrender to Jesus, who is the truth in person. Jesus said: *"I am the truth."* (John 14:6) And it means through the indwelling of Jesus to live according to God's word and directives, because He said: *"Your word is truth."* (John 17:17) and Psalm 119:142 says: *"Your law is truth."* If we don't have real worship now, then aren't we in danger of failing at a critical moment? This will be a big problem for all the carnal Christians.

I think we all want to make progress with God's help and to grow in knowledge. It may be that the following false belief was a hindrance for some in moving forwards.


## BAPTISM AND THE HOLY GHOST

Some people think they are filled with the Holy Ghost because they are baptized and thus everything is ok and they don't need to do anything more. D. L. Moody commented on this: "Many think that because they were filled once that they are filled forever. Oh my friend, we are porous vessels; it is necessary for us to constantly remain under the fountain in order to be full." [60]

Joseph H. Waggoner said:

**"In all cases, where baptism is seen as proof for the gift of the Holy Spirit, the repentant sinner is lulled into carnal security.** He solely trusts on his baptism as a sign of God's grace. Baptism and **not the Spirit in his heart** will be his sign or 'testimony' ..." [61]

---

60  D. L. Moody, *They Found the Secret*, p. 85, 86; quoted in *"10 Days – Prayers and Devotions ..."* by Dennis Smith, p. 23

61  Joseph H. Waggoner, *The Spirit of God* (Battle Creek, Michigan 1  877), p.35f, quoted in Garrie F. Williams, *Erfüllt vom Heiligen Geist* (Lüneburg, 2007), S. 58

Baptism is definitely a significant decision; this corresponds to God's will. It has and will keep its great significance. But we shouldn't look back to an event in the past as proof that we are filled with the Holy Ghost. Instead we should know **now** and experience **now** that we are filled with the Holy Ghost.

Some people received the Holy Ghost **before** they were baptized – for example Cornelius and his household or Saul. Others received the Holy Ghost **after** they were baptized – for example the Samaritans or the 12 men in Ephesus. But it is all the same if a person received the Holy Ghost **before, at or after** baptism: what matters is that we received the Holy Ghost at some time and that we have Him in our hearts **now**. It isn't crucial what happened in the past, but rather how things are now – today.

I want to remind you again: We received our physical lives at birth. Our life is maintained by daily food, drink, exercise, sleep, etc. otherwise we wouldn't live very long. The same laws apply to our spiritual lives as to our physical lives. We received new life through the Holy Ghost, namely when we completely surrendered ourselves to Christ. Our spiritual life is maintained through the Holy Ghost, prayer, the word of God, etc. E. G. White said: "The natural life is preserved moment by moment by divine power; yet it is not sustained by a direct miracle, but through the use of blessings placed within our reach. So the spiritual life is sustained by the use of those means that Providence has supplied." [62]

Neither the physical nor the spiritual life remains automatically in us. It is necessary to use the means that God has provided for us.

This means: When we are born again the Holy Ghost is given to us to stay. But in order for Him to stay it depends upon the daily use of the means, which the Lord has provided us with. What result can we expect if we don't use the "means"?

The Holy Ghost is the most important of all these "means". In addition, prayer is very important, being connected to God through His word, taking part in the worship services and other things.

I think we can agree that as a rule it is also necessary to **daily** care for the inner person. If we don't do it, then we will experience regrettable consequences. We can neither eat ahead nor can we stock up on the Holy

---

62  E.G. White, The Acts of the Apostles (1911), p. 284.2

Ghost. "God does not bestow help for tomorrow." [63] I think it is reasonably clear that daily surrender to Jesus is necessary and that we should daily invite the Holy Ghost into our lives.

**Both of these matters serve the** *same* **purpose – they are two sides of the same coin;** having an intimate relationship with Christ. I give myself to Him through surrender and by asking for the Holy Ghost I am inviting Him into my heart. Among other Bible verses 1 John 3:24 (see also John 14:17, 23) shows us that Jesus lives in us through the Holy Ghost: *"And by this we know that He abides in us, by the Spirit whom He has given us."*

## THE EFFECTS OF THE HOLY SPIRIT

When the Holy Ghost is in me, then He accomplishes in me what Christ achieved. Romans 8:2 says: *"For the law of the Spirit of life in Christ Jesus has made me free from the law of sin and death."* We can explain the "law of the Spirit" as the manner in which the Holy Ghost works in a heart completely surrendered to God. Only the Holy Spirit can bring to life in me what Christ achieved. E.G. White explains it well: **"The Spirit was to be given as a regenerating agent, and without this the sacrifice of Christ would have been of no avail...** It is the Spirit that makes effectual what has been wrought out by the world's Redeemer. It is by the Spirit that the heart is made pure. Through the Spirit the believer becomes a partaker of the divine nature ... The power of God awaits their demand and reception." [64]

Thomas A. Davis describes this process as follows: "This means that even the effectiveness of Christ's work for people is dependent on the Holy Ghost. Without Him everything Jesus did on this earth – in Gethsemane, on the cross, the resurrection and His priestly ministry in heaven – would be unsuccessful. The outcome of Christ's work wouldn't be much more useful than that of some big world religion or ethical leader. But although Christ was much more than these, He couldn't save humanity alone through His example and teachings. To change people it was necessary to work in them. This work is done by the Holy Ghost, who was sent to do this in people's hearts, which Jesus had made possible." [65]

---

63  E.G. White, *The Desire of Ages*, (1898), p.313.4

64  E.G. White, *The Desire of Ages*, (1898) p. 671.2 and 672.1

65  Thomas A. Davis, *Als Christ siegreich leben*, (HW-Verlag), Seite 43 /
    How to be a victorious Christian, R&H.

Isn't this alone reason enough to see to it that you are filled with the Holy Ghost?

"When the Spirit of God takes possession of the heart, it transforms the life. Sinful thoughts are put away, evil deeds are renounced; love, humility, and peace take the place of anger, envy, and strife. Joy takes the place of sadness, and the countenance reflects the light of heaven." [66]

There are many other valuable results from a life with the Holy Ghost, but there are also great deficiencies and losses without Him. The difference between a life with and without the Holy Spirit will be dealt with in more detail in chapter 4.

## AM I FILLED WITH THE HOLY SPIRIT?

Please ask yourself the following questions about being filled with the Holy Ghost: [67]

- Are there any noticeable effects of the Holy Ghost in my life? For example, has He made Jesus real and great to you? (John 15:16)
- Am I starting to hear and understand the inner voice of the Holy Ghost? Can He lead me in the big and little decisions in my life? (Rom. 8:14)
- Has a new kind of love for my fellow man arisen in me? Does the Holy Ghost give me tender compassion and profound concern for people, who I wouldn't normally choose as my friends? (Gal. 5:22; James 2:8,9)
- Do I experience again and again how the Holy Ghost helps me to deal with my fellow men? Does He give me the right words to reach a person's heart, who has worries and cares?
- Does the Holy Ghost give me strength to share about Jesus and lead others to Him?
- Do I experience how He helps me in my prayer life and helps me to express the deepest feelings of my heart to God?

When we think about these questions, we see what a great need we have to grow in the Holy Ghost, to get to know Him better and to love Him more.

---

66  E.G. White, The Desire of Ages, (1898), p. 173.1
67  Catherine Marshall, Der Helfer (Erzhausen, 2002), p. 24

A brother wrote: My father and I have become reconciled. After studying *Steps to Personal Revival* and the *40 Days books* one and two, I had the wonderful experience of being filled with the Holy Ghost. It was especially exciting for me to experience how the Holy Ghost works and wants to work in every area of my life.

## RECONCILIATION BETWEEN FATHER AND SON

My relationship with my father was always somewhat complicated. My wishes and prayers during my childhood and youth were always that I would have a better relationship with my father. But it got progressively worse. Another six to seven years went by. God filled the great emptiness in my heart. While studying and praying for the Holy Ghost my wife and I had a lot of big experiences with God. We prayed for our family and especially for my father. During this time I received new power to love my father. I was able to forgive him for everything that hadn't gone well in our relationship since my childhood. My father and I are now friends. He also started to become more spiritual and also started telling other people about God. Now, two years later, the relationship to my father is still very good. I thank God for this experience. I used to feel so powerless and often alone. But since I have started to pray daily for the Holy Spirit, I am experiencing a new and wonderful type of life and relationship with God. (Name known by the editor.)

> Prayer: Lord Jesus, I thank you that you want to remain in me through the Holy Ghost. Thank you that through daily surrender our trust and love relationship is growing. Lord, help me to get to know the Holy Spirit and His work better. I long to know what He wants to do for me, my family and my church and how we can have the assurance that we can receive the Holy Ghost when we daily ask. Thank you for this. Amen

# SUPPLEMENT FOR EPHESIANS 5:18 –
## "BE FILLED WITH THE SPIRIT!"

We can already see in the English text in Eph. 5:18 that this appeal is made in the imperative. Further, we can see that this command is directed to everyone. And we can also see that it is our duty to seek the fullness of the Holy Spirit. But the original Greek text makes it even clearer.

Johannes Mager comments on this: "In the New Testament letters there is only one passage, which speaks directly about being filled with the Holy Ghost: 'Be filled with the Spirit.' (Eph. 5:18) In the books of Acts we find being imbued with the Holy Spirit is a gift, which is used to act in a powerful way in specific situations. However, Paul states being filled with the Holy Ghost as a commandment, which is independent from situations in life and applies to all Jesus' followers. This short, but important command is comprised of four crucial aspects.

1. The verb 'fill' *(plerein)* is used in the imperative form. Paul does not make a recommendation here or give a friendly piece of advice. He doesn't make a suggestion, that a person can accept or reject. He commands as an empowered apostle. A command always appeals to a person's will. If a Christian is filled with the Holy Ghost, then it depends to a large degree on himself. **Christians are subject to the command to strive to be filled with the Holy Ghost.** This is our responsibility as people to be filled with the Holy Ghost.
2. The verb is used in the plural form. The command isn't directed at a single person in the church, who has special duties. Being filled with the Holy Ghost isn't a privilege for a few favored people. **The call applies to everyone who belongs to the church – always and everywhere. There are no exceptions.** For Paul it was normal that all Christians should be filled with the Holy Ghost.
3. The verb is in the passive tense. It doesn't say: 'Fill yourselves with the Spirit!', but rather 'Be filled with the Spirit!' No person can fill themselves with the Holy Ghost. This is exclusively the work of the Holy Ghost. Herein lies His sovereignty. **But the individual should create the conditions so that the Holy Ghost can fill him. Without his active will the Holy Ghost won't work in him.**

4. In Greek the imperative is in the present tense. This imperative present tense describes an event that is constantly repeated in contrast to the imperative aorist tense, which describes a one-time action. According to this, being filled with the Holy Ghost isn't a one-time experience, but rather a recurrent and progressive process. **A Christian isn't like a vessel that is filled once for all time, but rather has to be constantly 'refilled'.** The sentence could be expressed this way: **'Let yourselves be consistently and repeatedly filled anew with the Spirit!'**

**Being filled with the Holy Ghost,** which was given to us at baptism [provided it was a baptism in water and Spirit with a complete surrender], **can be lost when the fullness that was given us isn't retained.** If it is lost, it can be gotten again. Being filled with the Spirit must be repeated so that the Holy Ghost can occupy all areas of our life and our spiritual life doesn't wilt feebly. Being filled with the Spirit doesn't mean that we quantitatively have more of Him, but rather that the Spirit has more and more of us. **That's why Paul commanded all the believers to be constantly filled with the Spirit.** This is a normal condition for a Christian. One baptism, but many 'fillings.'" [68]

**The Lord himself has given the command: \***
**Let yourselves be consistently and repeatedly filled**
**anew with the Spirit! \*\***

---

**68** Johannes Mager was a pastor, evangelist and for many years a university lecturer on systematic theology. Most recently, he was the head of the ministry department in the Euro-African Division in Bern, Switzerland (now the Inter-European Division). Presently he is retired and lives in Friedensau. The quote is from his book: *Auf den Spuren des Geistes*, (Lüneburg, 1999) page 100-101 (with permission from the publishing house)

\*    E.G. White, Mount of Blessing, MB 20.3 (egwwritings.org)

\*\*  Johannes Mager, *Auf den Spuren des Heiligen Geistes* (Lüneburg, 1999), Seite 101

# CHAPTER 4

# WHAT DIFFERENCES CAN WE EXPECT?

*What advantage do we have
with a life filled with the Holy Spirit?
What do we lose when we
don't pray for the Holy Ghost?*

## A COMPARISON BETWEEN CARNAL AND SPIRITUAL CHRISTIANITY

The consequences of carnal Christianity have already been partially listed for individual persons. Some of the consequences express themselves as follows:

- The person is not saved in this condition. (Rom. 8:6-8; Rev. 3:16)
- God's love – the agape love – isn't in the person (Rom. 5:5; Gal. 5:22); they are completely dependent on their human love; the lust of the flesh isn't broken. (Gal. 5:16)
- The person hasn't been strengthened with power through His Spirit. (Eph. 3:16-17)
- Christ doesn't live in this person. (1 John 3:24)
- The person hasn't received the power to witness for Christ. (Acts 1:8)
- The person acts in a human way (1 Cor. 3:3) that can easily cause rivalry and tensions.
- As a rule it is harder for this person to accept admonition.

- ▸ Their prayer life may be inadequate.
- ▸ The person only has human abilities to forgive and not to bear a grudge.

The carnal Christian acts at times like a natural man. Paul says: *"are you not carnal and behaving like mere men"* (1 Cor. 3:3 NKJV). Other times his actions are like those of the spiritual person, although he lives by his own power and abilities

**The spiritual Christian** experiences the fullness of God:

*"That He would grant you, according to the riches of His glory, **to be strengthened with might through His Spirit in the inner man,** that Christ may dwell in your hearts through faith; that you, being rooted and grounded in love, may be able to comprehend with all the saints what is the width and length and depth and height – to know the love of Christ which passes knowledge; **that you may be fill with all the fullness of God.** Now to Him who is able to do exceedingly abundantly above all that we ask or think according to the power that works in us, to Him be glory in the church by Christ Jesus to all generations, forever and ever. Amen."* Eph. 3:16-21 NKJV

## EFFECTS OF CARNAL CHRISTIANITY

I am sorry for the losses in my family and in my churches where I worked as a pastor as a result of my lack of the Holy Spirit. It is also true in this area that we can lead no one further than we are ourselves. We also need to realize that a personal deficiency of the Holy Spirit in individual persons in the family and church adds up or multiplies.

## Children and Youth

Carnal Christianity is a breeding ground for a liberal Christian life. People ignorantly try with good intentions to do what they can't do and then search for a way out. Is this the reason we are losing so many of our youth? Have we in ignorance or for other reasons set an example for our children and young people of carnal Christianity? As a result, did they become carnal Christians and hence have to struggle with discouragement? Is this the reason why many don't take it very seriously or don't come to church anymore or have left the church?

Not long ago an older brother told his church: "There is a reason for the problems we have today in our own lives and in the lives of our youth: the older generation has failed to understand the working of the Holy Ghost and to be filled by Him."[69]

May I remind you again of the consequence of lukewarmness (no complete surrender to Christ): "Halfhearted Christians are worse than infidels: for their deceptive words and noncommittal position lead many astray. The infidel shows his colors. The lukewarm Christian deceives both parties. He is neither a good worldling nor a good Christian. Satan uses him to do a work that no one else can do."[70]

However, if we live spiritually, we can show our children the way to God's help. Ellen White says something really amazing:

"Teach your children that it is their **privilege** to receive every day the baptism of the Holy Spirit. Let Christ find you His helping hand to carry out His purposes. By prayer you may gain an experience that will make your ministry for your children a perfect success."[71]

We taught our sons to pray. But did we teach them to pray daily for the Holy Ghost? Or didn't we know that ourselves? At that time my wife and I didn't know it. I am thankful that God overlooked this time where we lacked knowledge. But as a consequence how much loss occurred?

What wonderful children spiritual parents will have when they daily commit themselves to Jesus and pray for the Holy Ghost.

69  Garrie F. Williams, *Erfülltsein vom Heiligen Geist – Wie erfahren wird das?* (Lüneburg 2007), S. 8
70  EGW Letter 44, 1903, quoted in Adventist Bible Commentary, Vol.7, p.963 on Rev. 3:15-16
71  E.G. White, Child Guidance (1954), p. 69

## Atmosphere –
## Divine Love or only being nice to each other?

What difference is there in the atmosphere in marriages and families, church and fellowship with carnal or spiritual Christians, if the power of God is missing for a disciplined life, if God's love is missing and the power of sin isn't broken or if these things are present through God's grace?

Conservative carnal Christians tend to criticize. This isn't good. Although we have to talk about God's good directives, we should at the same time realize that essential change will only happen when the change comes from within.

Liberals tend to not take things seriously and adapt to worldly methods. God can't bless this either.

Joseph Kidder discovered the following general condition of the church today: "Lethargy, superficiality, worldliness, lack of generosity, ministers are burned out, teenagers are leaving the church, weak self-discipline, plans without any real background or result, a chronic lack of strong and dedicated men." [72]

The cause of our problem is the lack of our connection with Jesus (John 15:1-5) and too much trust in human efforts (Zach. 4:6). Kidder also sees the solution in a life filled with the Holy Ghost (Acts 1:8).

Jesus gave us a new command:
*"A new commandment I give to you, that you love one another; as I have loved you, that you also love one another. By this all will know that you are My disciples, if you have love for one another."* (John 13:34-35 NKJV)

To love as Jesus does means: to love with divine love (agape). We can only do this when we are filled with the Holy Ghost.

"Supreme love for God and unselfish love for one another – this is the best gift that our heavenly Father can bestow. This love is not an impulse, but a divine principle, a permanent power. The unconsecrated

---

72   Dr. S. Joseph Kidder, Anleitung zum geistlichen Leben (Andrews University), PPP Folie 3+4

heart [everyone, who isn't filled with the Holy Ghost, has one] cannot originate or produce it. Only in the heart where Jesus reigns is it found." [73]

I think there is a difference if we are "only" nice to each other or if we go beyond that and love with God's love. E.G. White gives us a significant clue:

"By putting on the ornament of a meek and quiet spirit, ninety-nine out of a hundred of the troubles which so terribly embitter life might be saved." [74]

God's word indicates in 1 Thess. 4:3-8 something about marital life. Among other things these verses speak about living in sanctification and respectability within marriage. It is contrasted to the passionate lust of the Gentiles. Since it mentions a life of sanctification three times and also having the Holy Ghost, we realize that a life with the Holy Ghost can and should change our marriage relationships as well. God meant for us to have great joy and fulfillment in our marital life. Doesn't this show us that God wants to help us deal with loving tenderness rather than with lust?

Jesus prayed for the unity of His disciples: *"That they all may be one, as You, Father, are in Me and I in You; that they also may be one in Us, that the world may believe that You sent Me."* (John17: 21 NKJV)

William G. Johnsson says: "Many Adventists still have to comprehend what it means to be one with Christ. In the past we have probably not attached enough importance to it or hitched up the horse at the wrong end." [75]

---

73   E.G. White, *Acts of the Apostles* (1911) p. 551.2
74   E.G. White, *Testimonies for the Church*, volume 4, p. 348.3
75   William G. Johnsson, Adventgemeinde in der Zerreißprobe, (Lüneburg 1996), p. 118

Christ is in us when we are filled with the Holy Ghost. Spiritual Christianity contributes to having our prayers answered by the Lord. E.G. White says: "When God's people are one in the unity of the Spirit, all of Phariseeism, all of self-righteousness, which was the sin of the Jewish nation, will be expelled from all hearts ... God will make known the mystery which hath been hidden for ages. He will make known what are the *riches of the glory of this mystery among the Gentiles; which is Christ in you, the hope of glory*' (Colossians 1:27)." [76]

## Corrective Counseling

Will there be an effect on corrective counseling when it is not done or hardly done with God's love? What decisions will a church make, which is composed largely of carnal Christians or that even has a carnal pastor or president? When I think back on my work as a pastor, then I have the impression that spiritual church members tend to bring fallen members back to reason. And when the person repents and confesses, then the counseling has fulfilled its purpose. Sometimes carnal Christians tend to use counseling as punishment and even misuse it to exercise power (Matt. 18:15-17; 1 Cor. 3:1-4; 2 Cor. 10:3; James v. 19).

## GOD'S PROPHETIC WORD FOR THE LAST DAYS

God has the custom of revealing important developments through His prophets (Amos 3:7). Thus He gave important prophetic messages for the last days through Ellen White. Since many things would be completely different than in past times, it was important and necessary to have relevant additional information from God. Today we would call it an "update". According to Ellen White these messages are relevant until Jesus comes again. Since her counsel includes lifestyle change, reproof, admonitions, etc. a spiritual person can more easily accept it than a carnal person. (But just because someone takes these counsels seriously, it doesn't automatically mean that they are spiritual.) It would be wise to think about the words in Deuteronomy 18:19 NKJV: *"And it shall be*

---

[76] E.G. White, Selected Messages, Book 1 (1958), p. 386.1

*"When God's people are one in the unity of the Spirit, all of Phariseeism, all of self-righteousness, which was the sin of the Jewish nation, will be expelled from all hearts."*

*that whoever will not hear My words, which He (the prophet) speaks in My name, I will require it of him."*

This shows us clearly that the message from a true prophet doesn't have to do with that person, but rather with God himself. How can we know if someone is a true prophet? God's Word gives us five test points. A true prophet must comply with all five points.

1. Their way of life – *"Therefore by their fruits you will know them."* Matt. 7:15-20
2. Fulfillment of prophecies: Deut. 18:21-22 (with the exception of conditional prophecies – for example Jonah.)
3. Call for loyalty to God (God's word). Deut. 13:1-5
4. Recognize Jesus as a true person and the true God. 1 John 4:1-3
5. Agree with the teachings of the Bible. John 17:17

All of God's commands, including His counsel through the prophets, are for our own good. That is why they are exceptionally valuable. Hence spiritual people can obey in God's power and with joy and know that it contributes to success in life. *"Believe in the Lord your God, and you shall be established; **believe His prophets, and you shall prosper."*** (2 Chron. 20:20b NKJV)

Our study guide to the Sabbath school lesson says the following about the relationship between a life with the Holy Ghost and the words of a true prophet: "Whoever rejects the prophetic word, closes themselves to the instruction of the Holy Spirit. The result today is no different than it was then – loss of a relationship with God and being open to negative influences."[77]

---

77 Studienanleitung Standardausgabe, Philip G. Samaan, 10.11.1989, to question 8

## PLANNING / STRATEGY

An important task is to search for good solutions and methods for the duties within the church and in mission work. It is a question of our plans and strategies. It mainly has to do with strengthening the church spiritually and winning more souls.

I have been baptized for 65 years and have been a minister for 43 years. We have developed an abundance of programs and methods. We were very industrious. In this context I have to think again about the words of Dwight Nelson at the General Conference session in 2005.

> "Our church has exhaustively developed admirable forms, plans and programs, but if we don't finally admit our spiritual bankruptcy [lack of Holy Spirit], which has taken hold of many of us ministers and leaders, we will never go beyond our pro forma Christianity."[78]

In the same tenor Dennis Smith says the following:

> "I have nothing against plans, programs and methods. But I am afraid that we often depend on these things to move God's work forward. Plans, programs and methods will not complete God's work. Great speakers, wonderful Christian concerts, satellite broadcasts won't end God's work. God's Spirit will end the work – God's Spirit that speaks and serves through Spirit filled men and women."[79]

## BAPTISM / WINNING SOULS

The Bible shows us that the Holy Ghost is a crucial prerequisite for winning people for Christ (see the book of Acts). In Germany we have on the one hand, churches which are growing and on the other hand, churches which are stagnant or shrinking. Worldwide the number of members in our church has grown twentyfold in the last 60 years. We can certainly list many reasons for this situation in Germany. But one thing is clear for me: The main reason is the lack of the Holy Spirit. Naturally this problem has intensely preoccupied us. We have developed or adapted many plans and programs. We have seen that a lack of the Holy Ghost in this great ef-

---

78  Helmut Haubeil (Hrsg.), Missionsbrief Nr. 34, (Bad Aibling, 2011) page 3
79  Dennis Smith, *40 Days – Prayers and Devotions to Prepare for the Second Coming* (Wien, 2012), p. 88

fort has led to a loss of funds and time since we pursued unnecessary or unsuccessful ways. Two quotes from E. G. White illustrate this situation:

> "The Lord does not now work to bring many souls into the truth, because of the church members who have never been converted and those who were once converted but who have backslidden. What influence would these unconsecrated members [carnal Christians] have on new converts?" [80]

> "If we would humble ourselves before God, and be kind and courteous and tenderhearted and pitiful, there would be one hundred conversions to the truth where now there is only one." [81]

On the other hand, we have baptism of people, who aren't prepared sufficiently. E. G. White said:

"The new birth is a rare experience in this age of the world. This is the reason why there are so many perplexities in the churches. Many, so many, who assume the name of Christ are unsanctified and unholy. They have been baptized, but they were buried alive. Self did not die, and therefore they did not rise to newness of life in Christ." [82]

This was written in 1897. What is the situation like today? The problem is: whoever isn't born again hasn't been filled with the Holy Ghost. Jesus said: *"Unless one is born of water and the Spirit, he cannot enter the kingdom of God."* (John 3:5 NKJV) Isn't it true that we meet with the lack of the Holy Ghost in every area?

## THE HOLY GHOST AND PREACHING

God tells us the following about the meaning of the Holy Ghost and **preaching:** "The preaching of the word will be of no avail without the continual presence and aid of the Holy Spirit. This is the only effectual teacher of divine truth. Only when the truth is accompanied to the heart by the Spirit will it quicken the conscience or transform the life. One might be able to present the letter of the word of God, he might be

80  E.G. White, *Testimonies for the Church* Vol. 6, (1901) p. 370.3
81  E.G. White, *Testimonies for the Church* Vol. 9 (1909), p. 189.4
82  E.G. White, MS 148 (1897)

familiar with all its commands and promises; but unless the Holy Spirit sets home the truth, no souls will fall on the Rock and be broken. No amount of education, no advantages, however great, can make one a channel of light without the co-operation of the Spirit of God."[83]

Preaching doesn't only take place during a sermon, but also in lectures, Bible studies or care groups.

> Randy Maxwell says:
> "But the truth is, we're dying of thirst for contact with the living God!"[84]

Is the lack of the Holy Spirit also the cause of fear? Could Emilio Knechtle be right when he says: "Why don't we succeed in turning this corrupt world upside down? Something has gone wrong with our convictions. We are afraid of conflicts, we are afraid of run-ins, we are afraid of difficulties, we are afraid of losing our job, we are afraid to lose our reputation, we are afraid to lose our lives. So we keep silent and hide. We are afraid to proclaim the gospel to the world in a loving and yet powerful manner."[85]

The solution to this problem is found in Acts 4:31 NKJV: *"And when they had prayed, the place where they were assembled together was shaken; and they were all filled with the Holy Spirit, and they spoke the word of God with boldness."*

## THE HOLY SPIRIT AND OUR LITERATURE

The following is said about our literature: "If the salvation of God is with the one that writes for the paper, the same spirit will be felt by the reader. A piece written in the Spirit of God angels approbate, and impress the same upon the readers. But a piece written when the writer is not living wholly for the glory of God, not wholly devoted to him angels feel the lack in sadness. They turn away and do not impress the reader with it because God and his Spirit are not in it. The words are good but it lacks the warm influence of the Spirit of God."[86]

---

**83** E.G. White, *The Desire of Ages* (1898), p. 671.4
**84** Randy Maxwell, *If my people pray ...* (Pacific Press, 1995), p.11
**85** CD *Die letzte Vorbereitung*, Teil 6
**86** E.G. White, *PH 016*, p. 29.1

> *I want to emphasize again: Naturally everything we did wasn't wrong. By no means. We have developed good and very good things; God certainly blessed our human efforts as far as possible. But the important question is: Do we approach these duties as spiritual or carnal Christians? One thing is certain: When we struggle to find solutions on a carnal basis, we will invest a lot of time in vain; we will perform many tasks, which will be of no use.*

## HOLY SPIRIT: NO FORMER RAIN, NO LATTER RAIN

"The former rain, being filled with the Holy Ghost, brings us the necessary spiritual maturity, which is essential so that we can benefit from the latter rain." [87]

"The latter rain, ripening earth's harvest, represents the spiritual grace that prepares the church for the coming of the Son of man. But unless the former rain has fallen, there will be no life; the green blade will not spring up. Unless the early showers have done their work, the latter rain can bring no seed to perfection."[88]

## THE HOLY SPIRIT AND BIBLICAL SANCTIFICATION

"This work (biblical sanctification) can be accomplished only through faith in Christ, by the power of the indwelling Spirit of God." [89]

## GREAT MISSION WORK WITHOUT THE HOLY SPIRIT?

Could great institutions, successful evangelistic programs and powerful mission strategies have been developed without the Holy Ghost? Andrew Murray, the great missionary to South Africa, knew that this scenario was very possible and, indeed, reality in most of Christendom when he wrote:

---

[87] Dennis Smith, *40 Days – Prayer and Devotions to Revive Your Experience with God*, Book 2, (Vienna, 2013), p. 175

[88] E.G. White, *The Faith I live By*, (1958), p. 333.3

[89] E.G. White, *The Great Controversy*, (1911), p. 469.3

"I may preach or write or think or meditate, and delight in being occupied with things in God's Book and in God's Kingdom; and yet the power of the Holy Ghost may be markedly absent. I fear that if you take the preaching throughout the Church of Christ and ask why there is, alas! so little converting power in the preaching of the Word, why there is so much work and often so little success for eternity, why the Word has so little power to build up believers in holiness and in consecration – the answer will come: It is the absence of the power of the Holy Ghost. And why is this? There can be no other reason but that the flesh [see Gal. 3:3] and human energy have taken the place that the Holy Ghost ought to have."[90]

## THE HOLY GHOST AND HEALTH

"I beseech you therefore, brethren, by the mercies of God, that you **present your bodies a living sacrifice,** holy, acceptable to God, which is your reasonable service." Rom. 12:1 NKJV

"Do you not know that you are the temple of God and that the Spirit of God dwells in you? If anyone defiles the temple of God, God will destroy him. For the temple of God is holy, which temple you are." 1 Cor. 3:16-17 NKJV

"Or do you not know that your body is the temple of the Holy Spirit who is in you, whom you have from God, and you are not your own? For you were bought at a price; therefore glorify God in your body and in your spirit, which are God's." 1 Cor. 6:19-20 (see also: Exodus 15:26)

People filled with the Holy Ghost are God's temple. Have you ever stopped to think what implications this has for your life? A temple is God's dwelling place. God said to Moses: "And let them make Me a sanctuary, that I may dwell among them." Exodus 25:8

If we take this statement seriously, then taking care of our health and our lifestyle will become a deliberate part of our discipleship. Our body belongs to God. Do you want to treat God's property carefully? Yes, we want to treat our bodies carefully and in fact according to God's instructions! This demands a certain amount of discipline. Someone, who is filled with the Holy Ghost, can and will usually implement this discipline with

---

90   Randy Maxwell, If My People Pray (Pacific Press 1995), p. 145

joy. The reward is better health in body, soul and spirit. Someone, who isn't filled with the Holy Spirit, will struggle and suffer disadvantages. God expects that we maintain the best possible health in body and spirit for His glory, for His service and for our own joy. In this area there is also no replacement for being filled with the Holy Spirit. When Jesus lives in us through the Holy Ghost, then He is also *"the Lord who heals you."* (Exodus 15:26) Healing is always the best for the person concerned and to God's glory. This can raise the question: Does the divine doctor heal everyone?

"An older Cambodian woman came as a refugee to the mission hospital, which was in a refugee camp in Thailand. She was dressed in the clothes of a Buddhist nun. She asked to be treated by Dr. Jesus. So they told her about Jesus. She placed her trust in Him and was healed body and soul. When she was able to return to Cambodia she was able to win 37 people for Christ."[91]

During loyal king Hezekiah's sickness the Lord sent him a message: *"Surely I will heal you."* (2 Kings 20:1-11) But why didn't the Lord heal him with a word, but rather gave him the task of putting on a fig poultice? Could it be that the Lord expects our participation through natural remedies or changes in our diet, exercise, rest, etc.? Why didn't God heal Paul and left him with a "thorn in his flesh"? Paul himself said: *"Lest I should be exalted above measure by the abundance of the revelations."* (2 Cor. 12:7-10) However E.G. White tells us: "The influence of the Spirit of God is the very best medicine that can be received by a sick man or woman. Heaven is all health; and the more deeply the heavenly influences are realized, the more sure will be the recovery of the believing invalid."[92]

Isn't it remarkable and significant what a certain business man wrote? He shared how all the health seminars hadn't done him any good. But since he started to daily pray for the Holy Ghost, he had completely shifted to a healthy lifestyle and had adopted a vegetarian diet.[93] Doesn't this show that being filled with the Holy Ghost can motivate us and give us strength along with joy to accept a healthy lifestyle?

**91** Author unknown, *Our Daily Bread – Worship book* (RBC Ministries), 26. Nov. 1993
**92** E.G. White, *Medical Ministries* (1932) p.12.3
**93** Email from 7.3.2013

A sister read this experience. She wrote: Through my complete surrender to Jesus, God changed my life completely in a moment. After my prayer of surrender I went into the kitchen the next morning, stood by the coffee machine, shook my head and said to myself: no, I don't drink coffee anymore. In the past this would have been unthinkable, because when I tried to quit drinking coffee, I had had horrible headaches for five days – these were strong withdrawal symptoms. This time I didn't even think about what consequences it would have for me. I only knew that I didn't want to drink coffee anymore. Today I have no more desire for coffee. [94] This was only one of many changes in her life. (I recommend the 5th *"Andreasbrief"* on victory over tobacco and alcohol for anyone who wants to be free from addictions. It explains in length the way to deliverance through prayer and promises (only available in German). [95])

**A life with the Holy Ghost will greatly promote health reform. It is a matter of health information linked with power to change.** Don Mackintosh, Director of Newstart Global, Weimar, CA, says:

"The real need of our day is not simply health education – we have excellent information. What is needed is health information coupled with power to put it into practice, which is the power to change." [96]

Dr. Tim Howe says:

"Health education alone is not medical missionary work. Health education does not provide healing any more than the law of God provides salvation. To realize health or salvation the transforming power of God must be experienced." [97]

Finally, I would like to ask the question: What about faith healings? Can any be expected without being filled with the Holy Ghost? (see Mark 16:17-18; James 5:14-16)

---

94  Email from November 18, 2014 from Sister M.
95  Andreasbrief Nr.5, Sieg über Tabak und Alkohol, www.missionsbrief.de – Andreasbriefe. Man kann ihn auch beziehen bei Wertvoll leben, Adventist Book Center und TopLife – Wegweiser Verlag.
96  Dave Fiedler, *D'Sozo*, (Remnant Publications), Forward
97  Dave Fiedler, *D'Sozo*, (Remnant Publications), Forward

# PREPARATION FOR JESUS' SECOND COMING

There is no substitute for intimate fellowship with Jesus through the Holy Ghost as preparation for the Second Coming (or dying in the Lord). When Christ lives in me through the Holy Ghost, then I am ready through His grace. Three areas can show this. (This is dealt with in detail in *Spirit Baptism and Earth's Final Events*, by Dennis Smith.)

## Personal Relationship to Christ

Jesus said: *"And this is eternal life, that they may know You, the only true God, and Jesus Christ whom You have sent."* (John 17:3 NKJV) »Know« has a deeper meaning in the Bible than it does today in the English language. It means a complete, mutual and loving commitment. It is only present in a life with the Holy Ghost. This thought is expressed in the following quote:

"We must have a living connection with God. We must be clothed with power from on high by the baptism of the Holy Spirit, that we may reach a higher standard; for there is help for us in no other way."[98] In the parable of the 10 virgins Jesus said to the foolish ones: *"I do not know you."* What was the reason? The lack of oil, which represents the lack of the Holy Ghost. (Matt. 25:1-13). The men, who crucified Jesus, had great knowledge of the Old Testament. But because of their false interpretation they didn't look for a personal relationship with Jesus.

Are we aware that the generation of the last days, due to the last day circumstances, will need an intimate connection to God?

## Righteousness by Faith

In God's last message to humanity in the three angels' message it has to do with the question of the proclamation of the "eternal gospel". (Rev. 14: 6-7) What is the essence of this message that the whole world should and will hear? It is righteousness by grace through faith in Jesus Christ alone (Eph. 2:8-9). Those, who proclaim this last day message with power, must experience the power of the message themselves. They have to know and experience righteousness by faith through Jesus

---

98 E.G. White, *Review and Herald*, April 5, 1892

alone as the forgiver and redeemer from sin. This is only possible in a life filled with the Holy Ghost through which Jesus Christ can enable our obedience. Jesus dwelling in us is shown by obedience to all of God's commands. The world will be illuminated with this message (Rev. 18:1).

## Love for the Truth

What effects will be present in our lives today with or without a life filled with the Holy Ghost in reference to **love for the truth, studying God's word and implementing the truth in our lives?** 2 Thess. 2:10 NKJV says, that *"... those who perish, because they did not receive the love of the truth, that they might be saved"*. Those, who cannot be misled, have the love of truth in their hearts. How do we get this love? We can only have it when Jesus Christ lives in us through the Holy Ghost. Rom. 5:5 says that the love in our hearts comes from the Holy Ghost. Eph. 3:17 tells us that we will be *"rooted and grounded in love"* through the Holy Ghost. In John 16:13 the Holy Ghost is called *"the Spirit of truth"*. This shows us clearly that it is necessary to be a spiritual Christian in order to have a love for the truth. Do we have problems today with the love for the truth, to God's word, to prophetic writings? Consider the times ahead of us: "Only those who have been diligent students of the Scriptures and who have received the love of the truth will be shielded from the powerful delusion that takes the world captive... Are the people of God now so firmly established upon His word that they would not yield to the evidence of their senses?"[99]

God doesn't ask if we have discovered all truth, but rather He asks if we love the truth.

## FRUIT OF THE SPIRIT OR WORKS OF THE FLESH

"The influence of the Holy Spirit is the life of Christ in the soul. We do not see Christ and speak to Him, but His Holy Spirit is just as near us in one place as in another. It works in and through every one who receives Christ. **Those who know the indwelling of the Spirit reveal the fruits of the Spirit ... "**[100]

---

99  E.G. White, *The Great Controversy* (1911), p. 625.3
100  Editor Francis D. Nichol, *Adventist Bible Commentary* Vol. 6 (Hagerstown, 1980), p. 1112

Gal. 5:22 NKJV: *love, joy, peace, longsuffering, kindness, goodness, faith-fulness, gentleness, self-control.* Eph. 5:9 NKJV: *all goodness, righteousness and truth.*

Gal. 5:16-21 NKJV shows us that the power of sin will be broken in us through the Holy Ghost.

> "... *walk in the Spirit, and* **you shall not fulfill the lust of the flesh.** *For the flesh lusts against the Spirit, and the Spirit against the flesh; and these are contrary to one another, so that you do not do the things you wish.* **But if you are led by the Spirit, you are not under the law.** (see also Rom. 7:23 + 8:1) "*Now the works of the flesh are evident, which are: adultery, fornication, uncleanness, lewdness, idolatry, sorcery, hatred, contentions, jealousies, outbursts of wrath, selfish ambitions, dissensions, heresies, envy, murders, drunkenness, revelries and the like; of which I tell you beforehand, just as I also told you in time past, that those who practice such things will not inherit the kingdom of God.*" (Gal. 5:19-21)

## SPIRITUAL GIFTS

"Under spiritual gifts we mean the gifts given by the working of the Holy Ghost, as they are listed in 1 Cor. 12:28 and Eph. 4:11: apostles, prophets, evangelists, pastors, teachers, miracle workers, healers, helpers, adminis-trators, a variety of tongues. These gifts play a part in 'the equipping of the saints for the work of ministry'. ... They validate the testimony of the church and give it leadership and guidance."[101] The Holy Ghost also gives other talents for specific purposes: "in knowledge and in all manner of workmanship" (Exodus 31:2-6) or architecture (1 Chron. 28:12, 19).

When we want to become Jesus' disciples we surrender to Him ev-erything we have and are. Hence all our talents and abilities, inherent as well as learned, are placed at His disposal. He can give us additional talents and/or He can refine and purify our natural abilities.

Can we have spiritual gifts when we have a lack of the Holy Ghost?

---

101  Hrsg. Gerhard Rempel, *Schlüsselbegriffe adventistischer Glaubenslehre* (Hamburg), p. 44

## GOD'S CHOICE OR THE PEOPLE'S CHOICE?

We have a worldwide democratic structure in the church. But it was never thought of as popular democracy. The real goal of our votes is that everyone personally listens to God's voice and casts his vote accordingly. By listening to God's voice it makes God's will known through the vote. We certainly pray before taking part in any board meetings. Often the opportunity is given before a vote is cast for personal prayer so that it becomes clear to each person how God wants them to vote. Nehemiah said: *"Then my God put it into my heart ..."* (Neh. 7:5) and E.G. White said about Nehemiah chapter 1: "And as he prayed, a holy purpose had been forming in his mind..."[102]

Will a carnal Christian hear God's voice? If he hasn't consciously and completely surrendered to the Lord, then he certainly won't get an answer (Ps. 66:18; Ps. 25:12). If someone, who is a carnal Christian, votes sincerely to the best of his knowledge, then humanly speaking it is ok. But the instant human agreements are made, it becomes manipulation and sin.

The leaders have a great influence on God's work. It definitely makes a big difference and can have major consequences if brothers and sisters are leading, who have been called by God or who have been chosen by a human vote.

While reading a book on prayer I realized that we may ask God to show us the way we should go. (Ps. 32:8) The quiet listening to God's voice changed my whole life. I tell about this experience in an article called "From Business Representative to Pastor" (only available in German).[103] There is also a good sermon to listen to from Kurt Hasel "How can I make the right decisions?" (also only available in German)[104] And there is also a profound sermon to read from years ago by Henry Drummond: "How can I know God's will?" (only available in German)[105]

Here is an experience that happened on October 23, 2014: The mission center "Country Life Institute Austria" in Carinthia, Austria (TGM-Trainingszentrum für Gesundheitsmission und Gesundheitszentrum

---

102 E.G. White, *Southern Watchman (www.egwwritings.org)*, March 1, 1904
103 www.gotterfahren.info – Gott verändert Leben – Vom Prokurist zum Prediger
104 www.gotterfahren.info – Wege zum Ziel: Gott erfahren – Gottes Botschaft für unsere Zeit – Thema Nr. 11
105 Missionsbrief.de – Predigten lesen – Henry Drummond: Wie erkenne ich den Willen Gottes? (Deutsch und Englisch)

Mattersdorferhof) was faced with a decision: Should we build an addition or not? There were a lot of things for it and against it. The crucial question was: What is God's will in the matter? We didn't discuss the pros and cons anymore, but rather prayed for ten days that the Lord would prepare us to hear His voice and that He would give us His answer at a prayer meeting on October 23 (after the Newstart guests had left) if we should build the addition or not.

The prayer meeting took place with more than 20 participants. After fellowshipping in prayer each person asked God in silence to tell him if they should build or not. The personal answers from God were shared with the group as follows: on a piece of paper they should write "+" when they should build, they should write "–" when they shouldn't build, they should write "o" when they had no answer and they should write a "?" together with the other symbol when they were unsure of the answer. The result was a sign of God's wonderful leading: There were 14 "+" (4 of these with "+?"), 6 "o" and 4 blank pieces of paper. (There were also 2 answers, which were unclear and not counted. Thus God's leading was very clear that we should build. I am convinced that we will directly seek God's counsel more and more in the last days.

Joel 2:28-29 indicates this. E.G. White comments: "We must individually hear Him speaking to the heart. When every other voice is hushed, and in quietness we wait before Him, the silence of the soul makes more distinct the voice of God. He bids us, 'Be still, and know that I am God'." Psalm 46:10"[106]

## MONEY

What differences are there between spiritual and carnal Christians in relation to gaining and dealing with money? Do we see ourselves as the owners of our resources or as God's stewards? "Love of money and love of display have made this world as a den of thieves and robbers. The Scriptures picture the greed and oppression that will prevail just before Christ's second coming."[107]

106 E.G. White, *The Desire of Ages* (1898), p. 363.3
107 E.G. White, *Prophet and Kings* (1917), p. 651.1

## GOD'S ANGELS PROTECT GOD-FEARING PEOPLE

God's angels protect God-fearing people. *"The angel of the Lord encamps all around those who fear Him, and delivers them."* (Psalm 34:7 NKJV) "A guardian angel is appointed to every follower of Christ. These heavenly watchers shield the righteous from the power of the wicked one."[108] – When it talks about God-fearing people, followers of Christ and righteous people being under God's protection, does this mean that it applies to anyone who sees themselves as a Christian? Does it also apply to those who haven't completely surrendered their lives to God? It is true for children, because Jesus said in Matt. 18:10 NKJV: *"Take heed that you do not despise one of these little ones, for I say to you that in heaven their angels always see the face of My Father who is in heaven."* David, who completely entrusted his life to God, knew that he had no grounds for fear. He said: *"The Lord is my light and my salvation; Whom shall I fear? The Lord is the strength of my life; Of whom shall I be afraid?"* (Psalm 27:1 NKJV)

(I recommend that you read in the book *The Great Controversy* in chapter 31 the section about the ministry of the good angels. This is a great joy for every child of God.)


## CLOSING REMARKS

We have only touched on a few areas. There are still many areas of life and faith which could be added. For all of them the following is true:

*When we review the differences now, then there is not a single area that doesn't have major advantages through a life with the Holy Ghost. And the other way around, there isn't a single area where we don't have great disadvantages with a life without the Holy Ghost. Shouldn't this be a great motivation for us to daily dedicate our lives to God and to ask to be filled with the Holy Spirit?*

---

108 E.G. White, *The Great Controversy*, (1911), p. 512.2

"Some years ago a Boeing 707 took off from the Tokyo airport headed for London. It had a great take off. There was a clear, sunny sky. Soon the passengers could see the famous Mount Fuji in Japan. All of a sudden the pilot had the idea to circle around the mountain so that the passengers could enjoy this rare view.

He left the designated course of flight and changed over to visual flight. During visual flight the pilot dispenses with the security of the ground control center and depends completely on what he sees. The pilot saw the mountain close under him. His altimeter showed 4000 meters. What he didn't see was the fall winds and gusts of wind, which raged around Mount Fuji. The Boeing 707 was no match for the winds. The plane broke in the air, crashed and all of the passengers died."[109]

The carnal Christian lives in "visual flight mode". He makes all the decisions himself In spite of the best intentions he will fail. The spiritual Christian lives through the Holy Ghost in a loving and trusting relationship with His Lord, who leads him to a safe destination.

Prayer: Father in heaven, thank you that the indwelling of Jesus through the Holy Ghost makes such a positive difference in us and in our work. Please open my eyes even more to the work of the Holy Spirit. Please give me this fullness of life through Him, which Jesus wants to give us. Please help me to discover the key to solving this problem in the next chapter and to put it into practice. Thank you. Amen.

---

[109] Kalenderzettel February 17, 1979 by Reinhard Petrik

# CHAPTER 5

# THE KEY TO PRACTICAL EXPERIENCE

*How can I implement and experience God's solution for me? How should I pray so that I am sure of being filled with the Holy Spirit?*

## PRAYER AND BEING FILLED WITH THE HOLY GHOST

It is important that we go on this journey through faith and that we ask with faith for the Holy Ghost. That means that after praying for the Holy Ghost we need to trust and be certain that the Lord answered our prayer and that He already gave us the Holy Spirit while asking.

Gal. 3:14 NKJV says: *"...that we might receive the promise of the Spirit through faith."* Another translation (NIRV) says: *"...that we might receive the promise of the Holy Spirit by believing in Christ."*

God has given us a great help so that we can easily trust our heavenly Father. We call it **"praying with promises"**.

## PRAYING WITH PROMISES

First, here is a helpful example: Let's assume that my child isn't good in French at school. I want to encourage my child to study French hard. I promise him that if he gets a good grade on his report card that he will receive $20 from me. The child starts to study hard. I also help him with French and he really does get a good grade. What happens now? When the child comes home from school and comes through the front door he calls loudly: "Dad, $20!" Why is he so certain that he will get $20? Because a promise had been made and he has fulfilled the requirements. In fact, this is normal for most people today.

But it could be that at that moment I don't have $20. Can it be that God doesn't have something that He has promised? Impossible!

Or it could be that I take my promise back and say: "I read in a book on education that you shouldn't motivate children to study with money. So I can't give you the $20." Does God change His mind later? Impossible!

We can see that when we have a promise from God and have fulfilled the requirements, then there is only one possibility – that we receive the promise.

Through God's promises He wants to encourage us to go in a certain direction – for example receiving the Holy Ghost, which gives us God's power in our lives. He wants to make it easy for us to trust Him. Trust is at the heart of faith.

Now we want to read some key Bible verses in 1 John 5:14-15 NKJV for praying with promises:

*"Now this is the confidence that we have in Him, that **if we ask anything according to His will, He hears us.**"*

God gives a general promise that He answers prayers that are according to His will. God's will is expressed in commandments and promises. We may rely on them in our prayers. Then in verse 15 it goes on to say:

*"And if we **know** that He hears us, whatever we ask, **we know that we have the petitions that we have asked of Him.**"*

Another translation (NIRV) says:

*"If we know that God hears what we ask for, **we know that we have it.**"*

What does that mean? Our prayers according to God's will are answered **in the same moment that we bring them to God.** But emotionally we usually don't notice anything. Our prayers are answered by faith, not by our feelings. The feelings will come later on.

In praying with nicotine and alcohol addicted people I have learned: At the moment when they pray for deliverance they don't notice anything. They receive the answer by **faith.** But a few hours later they notice that they don't have any craving for tobacco or alcohol anymore. At this moment they have received the **practical** answer to their prayer.

Jesus said in Mark 11:24 NKJV: *"Therefore I say to you, whatever things you ask when you pray, believe that you **receive** them, and you will have them."*

E.G. White said: "We need look for no outward evidence of the blessing. The gift is in the promise, and we may go about our work assured that what God has promised He is able to perform, and that **the gift, which we already possess, will be realized when we need it most."**[110]

So we shouldn't be searching for outward proof. Here it certainly means searching for an emotional experience. Roger J. Morneau said: "The spirits [demons] would encourage people to listen to their feelings instead of the word of Christ and His prophets. In no surer way could the spirits obtain control of people's lives without the individuals realizing what was happening."[111]

Praying with promises opens God's treasury for us. Our loving heavenly Father opens an inexhaustible account for us. "They (the disciples) may expect large things if they have faith in His promises."[112]

## TWO GROUPS OF PROMISES

At the same time it is important to make a careful distinction between the promises in the Bible: **"The spiritual promises** – for forgiveness of sin, for the Holy Spirit, for power to do His work – **are always available** (see Acts 2:38-39). But the promises for temporal blessings, even for life itself, are given on occasion and withheld on occasion, as God's providence sees best."[113]

An example: Isa. 43:2 NKJV *"When you walk through the fire, you shall not be burned, nor shall the flame scorch you."* God kept this promise in a wonderful way for the three friends in the fiery furnace (Dan.3).

110 E.G. White, *Education* (1903), p. 258.2
111 Roger J. Morneau, *A Trip into the Supernatural,* Review and Herald 1982, p. 43
112 E.G. White, *The Desire of Ages,* (1898), p. 668.1
113 Morris L. Venden, *95 Theses on Righteousness by Faith,* (Pacific Press 1987), p. 60

But on the other hand, the reformers Hus and Jerome were burned at the stake in Constance. We could say that their prayers weren't answered. But nevertheless, weren't they answered in a fashion that we aren't acquainted with? Why? A papal writer described the death of these martyrs as follows: "Both bore themselves with constant mind when their last hour approached. They prepared for the fire as if they were going to a marriage feast. They uttered no cry of pain. When the flames rose, they began to sing hymns; and scarce could the vehemency of the fire stop their singing."[114] If someone is burned, they can only scream. Their behavior shows that God did intervene, just not in the manner which is readily visible for us. This shows me that the temporal promises still have significance for us.

## THANKING FOR THE ANSWER

Now for another important aspect: When our requests have been granted at the moment we asked, then it is right to thank God for the answer in the next. **Our thanks at this moment expresses our trust in God** that He has answered our prayer and that we expect it to be fulfilled when we need it most. Some believers notice something immediately after they pray. But for many believers it is similar to Elijah's experience: The Lord wasn't in the storm, in the earthquake or in the fire, but rather in the still, small voice (1 Kings 19:11-12). This was also my experience.

After a long period of time I thought nothing had happened. Then I suddenly noticed that many things had taken place in me without me realizing it.

## CHANGE MY THINKING

This means: **It is necessary to change my thinking at this moment:** *"... but be transformed by the renewing of your mind..."* (Rom. 12:2 NKJV)

Now it is correct to say: Thank you that you answered my prayer. Thank you for already granting my request. Thank you that I will experience it at the right time.

---

114 E.G. White, *The Great Controversy*, (1911), p. 109.3 Neander, "Kirchengeschichte", 6.Per., 2. Abschnitt, 2. Teil, §69; Hefele „Konziliengeschichte" Bd. VI, S.209 f

**This is not self-manipulation.** With self-manipulation I am trying to persuade myself. When I have prayed with a promise, then I have a divine basis for my changed thinking, because I have already been answered through faith. In this case, if I don't change my thinking, then I am showing God I don't trust Him, but rather I am feeling-oriented. With this behavior I am making God a liar and will thus not receive anything.

It is also important that I act accordingly, even when I don't notice anything. God always integrates the necessity to believe. He wants us to trust Him. Think about the crossing of the Jordan River. The priests first had to step into the water and then the water divided. Naaman had to dip in the water seven times before he was healed.

Maybe you are saying: "I can't do that. I can't even imagine doing that." Please remember that there are a lot of things we can't explain. To this day, we don't know what electricity is, although we all use it. To this day, we don't know how children learn to talk. But they all learn it. "In the natural world we are constantly surrounded with wonders beyond our comprehension. Should we then be surprised to find in the spiritual world also mysteries that we cannot fathom?"[115]

Let's think about Prov. 3:5-6 NKJV: *"Trust in the Lord with all your heart, and lean not on your own understanding; in all your ways acknowledge Him, and He shall direct your paths."* Here we find clear prerequisites from God for this promise of directing our paths. Every prerequisite is also a commandment. If we aren't sure that we have fulfilled the prerequisite, then we may pray for willingness with the surety that the Lord will answer us immediately. "...but if you are 'willing to be made willing', God will accomplish the work for you ..."[116]

Something small that may help: Do we know what we are doing, when we have prayed with God's promise, have fulfilled the requirement and then doubt being answered? We are making God into a liar. Under no circumstances do we want to do that. In this case, pray: Lord, I believe, help my unbelief. Then trust!

*There is very valuable advice on praying with promises in the chapter "Faith and Prayer" in the book "Education" by E.G. White.*

---

115  E.G. White, *Education* (1903), p. 170.1
116  E.G. White, *Thoughts from the Mount of Blessing* (1896), p. 142.1

## PRAYING FOR THE HOLY SPIRIT

I think we have the best qualifications for praying to be filled with the Holy Ghost. But we shouldn't forget that it doesn't have to do with making God willing to do our will, but rather believing in His promises and His trustworthiness.

### Promise for Receiving the Holy Ghost

The Lord has given us wonderful promises for receiving the Holy Ghost:

> **Luke 11:13 NKJV:** *"If you then, being evil, know how to give good gifts to your children,* **how much more will your heavenly Father give the Holy Spirit** *to those who ask Him!"*

Hasn't our heavenly Father made a binding commitment here? The requirement in this wonderful promise is: ask! Yet Jesus doesn't mean asking one time, but making a constant appeal.

However, it is important to see the context here. We should also read the other texts, which speak about the same thing, for example:

> **Acts 5:32 NKJV:** *"And we are His witnesses to these things, and so also is the Holy Spirit whom God has given to those who obey Him."*

The requirement here is: **obedience!** We can see here that we can't support ourselves with only one text: we also have to consider the context of the promise. It doesn't have to do with being obedient once with something that is pleasant for us. Rather, it has to do with obeying Him: our wonderful redeemer and friend. Obedience creates joy. Pray every morning for an obedient heart. Pray that the Lord will make you willing to do everything He wants and will help you accomplish it. This creates a good prerequisite.

> **John 7:37 NKJV:** *"If anyone thirsts, let him come to Me and drink."*

Here it has to do with the **desire** for the Holy Ghost. If you have no desire, or think you have too little, then you may pray for desire. It is a request according to God's will, which will be immediately answered. When we ask our wonderful God He will create in us "the desire and the accomplishment". We may also pray for the desire for a close relationship with God, to love Him with our whole hearts, to serve Him with joy, to have a growing desire for Jesus and His soon return and reunion in God's kingdom, a desire to read God's word and to learn from it, as well as the desire to help and be equipped to help save the lost.

> **John 7: 38-39 NKJV:** *"He who believes in Me, as the Scripture has said, out of his heart will flow rivers of living water. But this He spoke concerning the Spirit, whom those believing in Him would receive."*

Here the condition is: **belief!** We see here that our faith in Jesus Christ, our trust in God, is an important prerequisite for receiving the Holy Ghost. But when we pray with promises, then believing is easy.

> **Gal. 5:16 NKJV:** *"I say then: Walk in the Spirit, and you shall not fulfill the lust of the flesh."*

We actually have a **promise** here, which is expressed as a command. When God wants me to walk in the Spirit, then that clearly means that He wants to fill me with the Holy Ghost. And He shows us here that when we are filled with the Holy Ghost, then we aren't at the mercy of our lusts anymore. The Holy Ghost breaks the power of sin in us (Rom. 8:1-17, especially v. 2). Through the Holy Ghost *"the deeds of our body"* are put to death (Rom. 8:13). Think of Paul, who said about himself: *"I die daily."* It is something tremendously valuable not to be at the mercy of the works of the body (Gal. 5:18-21), but rather to grow the fruits of the Spirit (Gal. 5:22).

We can compare sin not being able to invade our lives to the assembly of binoculars. In order for no dust to get into the lenses the room has to be accordingly over-pressurized. This means that the air moves outwards when the door is opened. No dust can enter. In the same way, when we are filled with the Holy Ghost, *"you shall not fulfill the lust of the flesh"*. (Additional information on this subject is in the section: *"Can a person remain spiritual?"* at the end of the chapter.)

> **Eph. 3:16-17&19 NKJV:** *"That He would grant you, according to the riches of His glory, to be strengthened with might through His Spirit in the inner man, that Christ may dwell in your hearts through faith; that you, being rooted and grounded in love... that you may be filled with all the fullness of God."*

Maybe we don't notice any of the power for a long time. It could be like it is in nature. In the winter the trees are bare and in spring green. There are tremendous powers at work in this revitalization. But we can't see or hear them. But then we see the results. That is the way it was for me. I thank God that He gives me abundant power.

Another example: We have known for a few decades that we have electric currents in our bodies. They are there. But we aren't aware of them.

> **Eph. 5:18 NKJV:** *"...be filled with the Spirit"* or *"let yourself be continually and repeatedly refilled with the Spirit".* [117]

> **Acts 1:8 NKJV:** *"But you shall receive power when the Holy Spirit has come upon you; and you shall be witnesses to Me ..."*

The disciples had the commission to wait until the power came. They didn't wait idly. "They prayed earnestly for the empowerment to meet people in their daily lives and to have the right words to lead sinners to Christ. They laid aside all their differences and aspirations to power." [118] We may also pray with this promise.

## NO POSITIVE RESULT ...?

"A young man was looking for counsel, since he wanted to be filled with the Holy Spirit. He was really struggling. The pastor asked him: 'Have you completely submitted your will to God?' 'I don't think I completely have.' 'Well', said the pastor, 'then it won't do any good to pray [to be filled with the Holy Ghost], till you have completely submitted your will to God. Don't you want to submit your will to God now?' 'I can't', he

---

[117] Johannes Mager, *Auf den Spuren des Heiligen Geistes*, (Lüneburg, 1999), Seite 101
[118] E. G. White, *The Acts of the Apostles*, p. 36-37

replied. 'Are you willing for God to do it for you?' 'Yes', he answered. 'Then ask Him to do it.' He prayed: 'Oh God, empty me from my own will. Bring me into complete submission to your will. Lay down my will for me. I pray in Jesus' name.' Then the pastor asked: 'Did it happen?' 'It must have', he said. 'I asked God for something according to His will and I know that He answered me and that I have that which I prayed for (1 John 5:14-15). Yes, it has happened – my will has been laid down.' Then the pastor said: 'Now pray for the baptism of the Holy Spirit [being filled with the Holy Ghost].' He prayed: 'Oh God, baptize me now with Your Holy Ghost. I pray in Jesus' name.' And it happened immediately when he laid down his will."[119]

## THE GREAT DIFFERENCE BEFORE AND AFTER

Even though I was acquainted with praying with promises for a long time and used it in special situations and experienced wonderful answers to prayer, I thought for many years that it was good enough if I just simply asked for the Holy Spirit in prayer without relying on specific promises. I know that many have the same opinion. I don't want to say that it is something wrong. But when I look back at my personal experience, then I can only regret that I only prayed this way without any promises. For a few years now I have been praying daily with promises for the Holy Ghost, so that after my prayer I have the assurance that I am now filled with the Holy Ghost. Through an experience on October 28, 2011 I realized the great difference in my life: before and after.

Since I have started praying with promises my relationship with God has become more intimate and Jesus is closer to me and has become greater to me. This isn't just a subjective feeling; I can link it to the following things:

▸ While reading the Bible I often have new and encouraging insights.
▸ In the battle with temptation I can remain victorious.
▸ My prayer time has become very precious to me and brings me great joy.
▸ God answers many of my prayers.

119 Reuben A. Torrey, *Der Heilige Geist – Sein Wesen und Wirken* (Frankfurt, 1966), p. 150

- I have greater joy and more *"boldness"* (Acts 4:31c) to tell others about Jesus.
- I have become more sociable with my own friends.
- I live happily through God's grace and feel secure in His hand.
- In a difficult phase the Lord sustained me in a wonderful way and strengthened me from within.
- I realized what spiritual gifts the Lord had given me.
- Criticism stopped. When I hear others criticizing I feel uncomfortable.

The change took place quietly. I noticed it first after I had spent some time daily praying for the Holy Ghost with biblical promises. Since then I am experiencing a different kind of Christianity. Previously my life with God was often laborious and difficult; now I experience joy and power.

I am sorry for the losses in my personal life because of the lack of the Holy Spirit, for the losses within my marriage and family and for the losses in the churches where I served as a pastor. When I realized this I asked the Lord for forgiveness.

It is unfortunately true in this area that we can't lead anyone further than we are ourselves. We also want to remember that the personal short-comings of individuals in the family and the church add up or multiply.

In order for others not to lament the same mistakes in their lives, I want to add a few thoughts.

In 2 Peter 1:3-4 it says that through an intimate relationship with Jesus we may *"through the ... great and precious promises ... be partakers of the divine nature"*.

This also means that the Holy Spirit is given to me through the promises. You can compare the promises to bank checks. When we present a signed check from an account holder, we can withdraw money from someone else's account. As God's children (John 1:12) we can daily withdraw with the checks (the promises) signed by Jesus. It wouldn't do any good to present our own checks, even if we had the checks made by an artist. We need the signed checks from the account holder.

There is another reason, which may encourage us to pray with promises. There is power in God's word. Why did Jesus pray on the cross three times with words from the Psalms? Why did He defend himself and rout Satan with Bible verses during Satan's temptations in the wilderness? (Matt. 4:4, 7, 10) He said: *"Man lives through **every word** that proceeds out of the mouth of God."*

Jesus, the creator, knew that there is power in God's word. "In every command and in every promise of the word of God is the power, the very life of God, by which the command may be fulfilled and the promise realized." [120] What a wonderful statement! The power of God and His life are in every promise. When we pray with promises we are using God's word in our prayer. It says about God's word: *"So shall My word be that goes forth from My mouth; it shall not return to Me void…"* (Isaiah 55:11 NKJV)

I plan only to pray for the Holy Ghost with promises. When praying with promises I know that after I have asked for the Holy Ghost that I have received Him based on the promise in God's word in 1 John 5:15 NKJV: *"And if we know that He hears us, whatever we ask, **we know that we have the petitions that we have asked of Him.**"* When I pray without a promise, then I **hope** that my prayer will be answered. It's better to take the time for a prayer like this and experience a blessed day, rather than to complain about failures in the evening.

I received an email, which was written with great joy: "I never thought it was possible that it would make such a big difference if I prayed for God's leading throughout the day with 'my own words' or if I prayed with promises from the Bible! Promises have always been very important to me. I have always believed in them, but I failed to claim them daily. My life with Jesus has gained a deeper, more joyful, more confident and calmer dimension. I thank God for this."[121]

For this reason, I have decided to share an example of a prayer for the Holy Ghost with promises. Naturally, it can be shortened. It is important that we learn to pray for ourselves directly from God's word. But the vital point is that our faith is strengthened by the promises in such a way that after we have prayed we have the assurance that we have received the Holy Ghost. We receive the Holy Ghost when we believe what we pray.

---

120 E.G. White, *Christ's Object Lessons* (1900), p. 38.2
121 Email to H. Haubeil C.S.

# A MODEL PRAYER WITH PROMISES FOR THE DAILY RENEWING OF THE HOLY SPIRIT

*Father in heaven, I come to you in the name of Jesus our Savior. You said:* **Give me your heart.** *(Prov. 23:26) I want to do that now by submitting myself to you today with everything I am and have.*[122] *Thank you that you have already answered this prayer according to Your will, because Your word says that if we pray according to Your will we know that we have already received it (1 John 5:15). And you also said that you would by no means cast anyone out who comes to you (John 6:37).*

*Jesus said: "If you then, being evil, know how to give good gifts to your children, how much more will your heavenly Father give the Holy Spirit to those who* **ask** *Him." (Luke 11:13)*

*You further said that you would give the Holy Ghost to those, who* **believe** *in you (John 7:38-39), who obey you (Acts 5:32), who let themselves be renewed with the Holy Spirit (Eph. 5:18) and who* **walk in the Spirit** *(Gal. 5:16). This is my desire. Please accomplish this in me. For this reason I sincerely ask you Father to give me the Holy Ghost today. Since it is a request according to Your will, I thank You that have given me the Holy Ghost now (1 John 5:15). Thank You that I have received Your divine love at the same time, because Your word says:* **"The love of God has been poured out in our hearts by the Holy Spirit."** *(Rom. 5:5; Eph. 3:17) I want to say with the psalmist:* **"I will love You, O Lord, my strength."** *(Psalm 18:1) Thank you that I can love my fellow human beings with Your love.*

*Thank You that through the Holy Ghost the power of sin has been broken in me (Rom. 8:13, Gal. 5:16). Please save and protect me today from sin and from the world, give me protection from the fallen angels, save me from temptations and when necessary snatch me and save me from my old corrupt nature. (1. John 5:18)*

---

122 "Only those who will become co-workers with Christ, only those who will say, Lord, all I have and all I am is Thine, will be acknowledged as sons and daughters of God." E.G. White, *The Desire of Ages* (1898), p. 523.1

*And please help me to be Your witness in word and deed (Acts 1:8). I praise You and thank You for hearing my prayer. Amen.*

Jesus himself wants to live in us through the Holy Ghost (1 John 3:24; John 14:23). E.G. White said: "The influence of the Holy Spirit is the life of Christ in the soul."[123] The power that changed Peter, Paul and many other people is also available to us. He also gives us *"that He would grant you, according to the riches of His glory, to be strengthened with might through His Spirit in the inner man".* (Eph. 3:16)

Being filled by the Holy Ghost is the key to a life of faith in joy, power, love and victory over sin. *"... where the Spirit of the Lord is, there is liberty."* 2 Cor. 3:17b

In a message I received it said the following: "Many church members daily pray the suggested prayer in twos. For the last five months I have been praying it with my girlfriend. Not only is everything progressing in personal areas, but also in the home, relationship, marriage, spiritually and in church – not in a manner that causes great conflicts, but rather it happens in a quiet, natural way. We are amazed and see this as God's clarification process, which can make life easier in ways, since we feel God's closeness more and more. "[124]

## CAN A PERSON REMAIN SPIRITUAL?

Yes! When we don't allow an attitude of unbelief to develop and we breathe spiritually: *"exhaling"* by confessing our sins and *"inhaling"* by making use of God's love and forgiveness and by renewing our prayer of faith to be filled with the Holy Ghost.[125]

It is like the relationship to our children. When a child was disobedient, it still remains our child. But we feel a disruption in the relationship. The child may not be able to look us in the eye. This disruption is corrected by confessing.

But a person can naturally become carnal again in the long-run. The Bible doesn't speak about "once saved, always saved". Our sinful nature is still existent. "None of the apostles and prophets ever claimed to be without sin."[126]

---

123  Editor Francis D. Nichol, *Adventist Bible Commentary* Vol. 6 (Hagerstown, 1980), p. 1112
124  Email to Helmut Haubeil: E.S.
125  Helmut Haubeil & Gerhard Padderatz, *Gott, Geld & Glaube* (Eckental, 2009), p. 97
126  E.G. White, *The Acts of the Apostles* (1911), p. 561.1

But through a life with the Holy Ghost and with Jesus in our hearts the power of sin is broken so that we can live a happy and strong Christian life. Our righteousness is only in Jesus Christ *"... who became for us wisdom from God – and righteousness and sanctification and redemption"* (1 Cor.1:30 NKJV). This important topic will be dealt with in more detail shortly.

If we have become carnal again by a lengthy neglect of the spiritual life or by the failure to breathe spiritually, then we can know that a compassionate redeemer is waiting for us.

It is important that we know the way that we can be renewed by God's grace and hopefully lead a spiritual life forever. No one need remain carnal.

But remember both personally and in general what Randy Maxwell said: "Do we think that the resuscitation of God's church from near spiritual death can be accomplished without effort?"[127]

The abundant life here and eternal life, the salvation of many people and our thanks for Jesus' great sacrifice is worth the effort. The crucial thing is meeting our Lord in the morning for worship. It is here that He equips us with power.

We read the following about the apostle John:

"Day by day his heart was drawn out toward Christ, until he lost sight of self in love for his Master. His resentful, ambitious temper was yielded to the molding power of Christ. The regenerating influence of the Holy Spirit renewed his heart. The power of the love of Christ wrought a transformation of character. This is the sure result of union with Jesus. When Christ abides in the heart, the whole nature is transformed."[128]

*"Open my eyes, that I may see wondrous things from your law."* (Psalms 119:18 NKJV) Thank You that you are leading me and I can say: *"I rejoice at Your word as one who finds great treasure."* (Psalms 119:162 NKJV)

---

127  Randy Maxwell, *If My People Pray* (Pacific Press,1995), p. 158
128  E.G. White, *Steps to Christ* (1892), p. 73.1

# CHAPTER 6

# WHAT EXPERIENCES LIE AHEAD OF US?

*Personal experiences, as well as experiences from churches, a conference and a union*

## THE EXPERIENCE OF A BROTHER

"For the past two years I have been praying daily for the outpouring of the Holy Ghost in my life. My request is that Jesus will thus live in me in greater abundance each day. My walk with God [during this time] has been unbelievable. The fruit of the Spirit in Galatians 5 has become more visible in my life since I ask Jesus to live in me, to do His will in me and to daily renew me with the Holy Ghost. I have greater joy in reading the Bible, sharing Christ with others and I have a strong desire to pray for others; furthermore, my life-style has changed dramatically. I see this all as a confirmation of my daily search for God and my daily request for the Holy Ghost." C.H.  He shared further:

*"I challenge you to pray daily to be filled with the Holy Ghost for six weeks and see what happens."*

## 40 DAYS OF PRAYER IN SERBIA

"In September 2010, we translated and published the book *40 Days: Prayers and Devotions to Prepare for the Second Coming*. We made it available to all church members in our union. Then we organized weekly and daily prayer meetings during the following 40 days in local churches and in members' homes, where people fasted and prayed for a fresh outpouring of the Holy Spirit.

As this happened, a completely new climate began to develop in the local congregations. Inactive church members have become active and more interested in serving others. Those, who fought with each other for years over different issues (and had even stopped talking with each other!), reconciled, and began making plans for community outreach together.

Then in October 2010, during the Annual Council, "the Revival & Reformation initiative" was introduced. We gladly accepted it, seeing it as a continuation of what God had already started in our Union.

We have seen closer fellowship, greater unity and better common understanding among the Union officials as immediate results of these prayer meetings." [129]

## 40 DAYS OF PRAYER IN ZURICH / SWITZERLAND

"Our pastor and I each received independently from each other a book, which contents thrilled us. Its title is: *40 Days: Prayers and Devotions to Prepare for the Second Coming* by Dennis Smith, Review and Herald Publishing Association. This book can't be read and then just set aside. The contents changed my life.

Since our church in Zurich-Wolfswinkel (with about 100 members) sensed a great need for revival and prayer, we planned 40 Days of Prayer for the fall of 2011. The book gave detailed and valuable information for this and in addition, 40 appropriate daily worships.

The topics deal with being filled by the Holy Ghost, prayer, preaching, the life of Jesus and spiritual fellowship.

So we started our 40 Days on October 1, 2011 with great anticipation and expectation. Fortunately, most of the church members took part. Prayer partners met to pray daily, text messages were sent daily and people prayed over the phone every day. One group met every morning at 6 a.m. for worship and prayer.

---

129 M. Trajkovska, Southern European Union, Belgrade, quoted in *www.revivalandreformation.org*

Our 40 Days were an unforgettable experience. God answered many of our prayers, especially in connection with a series of lectures on biblical prophecy, which took place at the same time. These lectures were a great blessing. We had many visitors and 20 people registered for the following prophecy seminar. (Follow-up in March 2013: Between 50-60 guests came, which hasn't happened in Zurich in 20 years.)

God's Spirit has made ongoing changes in our church and it is a joy to see how our small groups are starting to grow and how church members, who are eager to give Bible studies, find interested people. Those who participated now have a deep desire for the continuation of the work of God's Spirit. We want to thank Him from our whole hearts and give Him the glory." Béatrice Egger, from the Adventist church in Zurich-Wolfswinkel.

## 40 DAYS OF PRAYER AND EVANGELISM
## IN COLOGNE / GERMANY

Pastor Joao Lotze is German-Brazilian. He worked for 38 years in churches and hospitals in Brazil, as well as in a union and the South American Division. He retired in March 2012. He and his wife agreed to come to Cologne as "His Hands Missionaries" and work in the Portuguese and Spanish speaking churches.

"We started in Cologne with small care groups to encourage the church members and to invite guests. Based on our experiences in Brazil we carried out 40 Days of Prayer in Cologne. The materials were available in Portuguese.

The churches with Portuguese, Spanish and German speaking members joyfully started the 40 Days of Prayer. We prayed daily for 100 friends and acquaintances. These peoples' names were written on a black board in the church. Not until we had reached the 30th to 35th day of prayer did we let these people know we were praying for them and at the same time invited them to a special Sabbath service for guests. 120 people came to this special church service. Christian Badorrek, the director of Personal Ministries for Nordrhein-Westfalen, held the sermon. Some of the guests cried with joy when they saw their names on the board.

Afterwards, Antonio Goncalves, an evangelist from Brazil, held an evangelistic series for 15 days. Each evening he spoke for 1,5 hours (with translation). The title of the series was: 'Let the Bible surprise you'. The topics had to do with the second coming, as well as topics from Daniel and Revelation. The lectures and the songs were translated from Portuguese into German. There were small choirs and good music each evening. Every evening closed with an altar call. We are thankful for the good reactions. The church members prayed intensively, especially for the people from the 40 Days of Prayer.

Our church sanctuary seats 80 people. But more than 100 people came. On the weekends the church was full and during the week there were about 60 people. 32 guests attended regularly. This led to 8 baptisms and 14 people joining the baptismal class. By the end of the year 13 people were baptized.

We have had many surprising experiences. It was difficult to find a translator. A catholic teacher offered to help. But she didn't have much experience with the Bible. Then we prayed for a protestant translator. Soon afterwards we got to know a lady in a restaurant, who explained that she translated with great joy from Portuguese to German in the Pentecostal church. She was our translator for the evangelistic series and she was also baptized.

Maria, the translator, asked if she could invite her friend Elisabeth to come. She is the leader of a small Columbian church in Cologne with 13 members. She came and brought members from her church with her. Since then two of these people have also been baptized. Elisabeth and her family are now receiving Bible studies.

Another experience is connected with the Hope Channel. A German woman found the Hope Channel by coincidence and was impressed by what she heard, including what was said about the Sabbath. She invited her husband to listen with her. He also enjoyed the messages. One day when they went to visit her mother, they were impressed to drive along another route. Along the way they saw a sign for a Seventh-Day Adventist Church. They realized they were the Adventists from Hope Channel. On Sabbath she went to the church service. Then she invited her husband and then her mother to join her. Since then all three of them have been baptized.

Another experience involves a Russian-German sister. She took part in the 40 Days of worship and started to pray for her Russian speaking neighbors. When she told one of her neighbors that she was praying for her, the neighbor was very surprised and said that she was looking for a church that kept the biblical Sabbath. She and other neighbors came to the evangelistic series. Two of them have been baptized.

Another experience involves a woman named Jeanne. She had been a member of the Baptist church in Brazil and now she was searching in Cologne for a Portuguese speaking church. She got in touch with the Adventist church, received Bible studies and was baptized. After her conversion she called her relatives in Brazil and told her uncle, who is an Adventist, that she is also an Adventist now. It was a big surprise for her mother, her siblings and the Baptist church in Brazil, which she had been a member of. Her family in Brazil subsequently visited an Adventist church to inform themselves about the Sabbath. This has led to five people being baptized in Brazil: her mother, two of her sisters and other relatives. Now she is praying for the conversion of her other sister, who lives in Argentina. She wants to be together with them in God's kingdom.

Under God's leading we have had many other experiences. At the first baptism eight people were baptized – one each from Italy, Germany, Peru, Brazil, Ukraine, Venezuela, Columbia and Russia.

In the fall we again had an evangelistic series in connection with the 40 Days of Worship. Jimmy Cardoso and his wife, who originally come from Brazil, but now live in the USA, held the evangelistic series. Although the series only lasted a week, we were able to baptize four dear people at the end. They had been having Bible studies previously. There were three Germans and one Italian.

Both of the baptisms were held in the main church in Cologne, which has 400 members and a beautiful baptismal facility.

We thank God that He surprised us in such a great way. I am convinced that He still has even greater experiences waiting for us. Please keep us in your prayers." João Lotze, Cologne, Germany


*Vital Intercession:* "I first just simply read the book [40-Days-Book] through. From the first page on I was very impressed. We shouldn't only pray for someone, but also affectionately care for them. This makes intercession come alive. Unfortunately, I had never seen intercession in this way before. Living out your faith! I am convinced that it is just as important for the person, who is praying, as it is for the person, who is being prayed for. Likewise, it convinced me from the start that the fellowship in the church would be strengthened. Oh, I hope that such fellowship will happen as it is described in the last chapters of the book. To be honest,

I had to cry, because I have yearned for such fellowship for a long time. I am convinced that the book 'Christ in me' nurtures us and frees us from our own accomplishments. I have read several books about 'Christ in me', but this book seems to be the most helpful. I believe that your prayer life will be strengthened by this book, that the fellowship in the church will be nurtured and that it will make intercession more alive. This book gives me hope for myself, for the church and for the world. I thank God for this book. Next, I plan to study the 40-Day guide book, pray over it and then take it wherever God shows me."

*A few weeks later* I received another email from this sister. "As you know I simply read the book through at first. But since I have started to study the worships with my prayer partner I have discovered that they are even more valuable than I thought at first. I have gotten answers to things, which I hadn't been able to on my own. Thank God for my prayer partner, who is participating intensively and actively." H.K.

*Not sure anymore:* "The booklet *Steps to Personal Revival* has touched me extraordinarily. ... Having been born in an Adventist family I believed I was taking the right path. The chapter on the ten virgins and especially Romans 8:9b: *"Now if anyone does not have the Spirit of Christ, he is not His"* really shocked me. I suddenly wasn't sure anymore if I had the Holy Ghost and if He was working in me, because I was sorely missing the corresponding 'fruits' in my life. This Sabbath afternoon I finished reading the booklet and a profound and fathomless sadness came over me. Then I read the prayer near the end of the book and a deep desire arose within me to receive the Holy Ghost, to let Him change my heart and that God would form me according to His will. ... A.P.

*Know HIM:* "Some time ago I read your article on revival. I have been preoccupied with this topic for about three years. Now, I just started to read *Steps to Personal Revival*. I can only say AMEN to it! I am glad that in these pages I found many of 'my own' thoughts. I am under the impression that in our church we are missing the goal by an inch. I can't shake off the feeling that we have lost sight of the essentials! Often it has to do with 'what is the truth', 'how we should live' or 'how important prophecy is', and I'm not saying this is wrong. But we overlook WHY God gave us these things! Doesn't the truth aim for complete fellowship with

God? Instead, shouldn't these areas help us REALLY get to know God? Isn't the aim of prophecy that we acknowledge God's greatness and omnipotence, that we understand that He holds the whole world in His hand and directs it and that in the same way He can lead and shape our lives? What is eternal life? John 17:3 NKJV: *'And this is eternal life, that they may KNOW You, the only true God, and Jesus Christ whom You have sent.'* In the parable the bridegroom simply says to the five foolish virgins: *'I know you not.'* The aim of our faith is to simply know God, to have fellowship with HIM, so that HE can fill us as He filled the temple back then (2 Chron. 5:13-14). And when He flows through us, fills our whole being, then we aren't living, but rather Christ is living in us." (Author known by editor)

## AMAZING ANSWERS TO INTERCESSION

"The second 40-Day book from D. Smith is an unbelievable blessing for me. Some of the people I have prayed for have experienced a 180° turnabout in their lives.

During the 40 Days I had a deep spiritual conversation with a friend. He told me that His life had taken a different course in the last few weeks. He had a greater need to pray, was reflecting more on God's word and was able to let things go that had been valuable and desirable to him before. I got up my courage and told him about the 40-Day book and also told him that he was one of the five people that I was praying for. Then he responded in positive surprise: 'So you are responsible for this whole thing.'

A girl made the decision to dedicate her life 100% to God. Although she had been a believer since she was a child, she had been living without God. She had no interest in faith and was completely ensnared in a worldly life. She has completely changed now; everyone, who knew her and sees her now, is amazed. She is studying the Bible with me now and is taking part in the 40-Day program in our church and wants to encourage others to have a more serious faith-life.

Another young girl, who I prayed for, had to take part in a week-long training course and had to stay in accommodations together with the other participants. She was worried about spending this time with all these strangers. One day before she left I encouraged her in prayer and told her that I had been praying for her for quite a while. So we prayed that God would give her peace in this situation and that He would make this experience an answer to prayer. During the training course she called me and excitedly told me that God had done something unbelievable with her. He not only had given her perfect peace, but He had also given her the courage not to take part in the evening amusements, which consisted of discos, alcohol, etc.

After the 40 days I have continued praying for these people, since I have heard and seen the great ways in which God answers prayer." A.M. (shortened version)


## HOW GOD WORKS THROUGH INTERCESSION

"In the last five years I had gotten completely out of touch with an important person to me. He seemed to ignore my messages. I had heard that he hadn't been going to church anymore over the past three years. (He had grown up in the church.) And that he was in a relationship with a non-Christian woman. I put this young man on my prayer list, even though I didn't think it would be possible to get back in touch with him, since he lived 600 km away and never answered me. Nevertheless, I prayed for a 'sign of life'.

On short notice I heard about the upcoming baptism of his brother, which 'just happened' to be taking place near me and was on a date during the 40-Days of Prayer (it had originally been planned for another date). I decided to attend – and met him! We were able to have a very deep discussion and he told me that for some time he had had an increasingly great need to come back to God, but that he didn't have the strength to change his lifestyle. I told him that for the past 20 days I had been praying intensively for him and that even before that he had been on my prayer list. He was speechless that exactly during this time he had felt God working on him.

During the very spiritual baptismal service he was very moved and when the pastor made an appeal, I could feel the battle that was taking place in him and after a long struggle he finally fell on his knees and started to cry. He surrendered himself to God again! At the end of the evening, he told me that he had decided to attend church regularly again and to change his lifestyle. He never expected this weekend to end in this way.

A few weeks later I met him at a youth mission conference, which again strengthened him and built him up. I thank God for the repentance of a beloved person." M.H.

## THE CHURCH IN LUDWIGSBURG / BADEN-WUERTTEMBERG, GERMANY

"At first we studied the 40-Day book as a couple and experienced great personal benefit and blessings during the time of prayer. Afterwards, we organized a prayer meeting twice a week in the church and read the book with the church members. We distinctly experienced God's blessing and leading and experienced many miracles during the 40 days. As a church God refreshed and revived us: church members, who had never had the courage to speak with strangers, suddenly spoke with strangers by their own initiative. God is binding us as a church closer together through prayer together. We had the privilege of having special experiences in the intercession and support of the five people that we prayed for during the 40 days. God worked in a special way in these people's lives. Again and again people from the street suddenly appear on Sabbath in the church service. We are giving Bible studies to one of these families. They had gotten acquainted with the Sabbath through videos in the internet and the book *The Great Controversy* and had been searching for a church for some time." Katja and Christian Schindler, Seventh-Day Adventist Church in Ludwigsburg (shortened version)

## 40 DAY EXPERIENCE

"Everything started with a seminar on *Steps to Personal Revival*. At that time a desire grew within me to experience God in my daily life. Then I heard about the 40 days of prayer and worship. It was immediately clear to me – I wanted to experience this adventure. Actually, I didn't know what I was getting myself into. Finding a suitable prayer partner (which is part of the program) wasn't difficult. The challenge for me was to find time for each other every day for 40 days. As a nurse I have very irregular working hours. I hadn't even thought about that. Nonetheless, God blessed my decision from the very start. With longing I waited for those precious minutes of the day in which we could share with each other about the topic and plead for the Holy Ghost. We discovered that the prayers changed something in our lives. And we couldn't keep it to ourselves. With every opportunity that came we felt impressed to share something. It was important to me to motivate other people to have the same experience. The effect didn't fail to appear. Some church members were infected with our enthusiasm. Quickly new worship pairs got together. We looked forward to sharing every week what we had experienced. This 'virus' was also caught by quite a few of our youth. The 40 Days ended much too quickly. We didn't want to and simply couldn't stop. So we continued our worship time with the book *Maranatha – The Lord is coming* by Ellen White. And God didn't make us wait for long. Still during the 40 days He gave us many wonderful answers to prayer. Someone, who we had prayed for during this time, came into contact with the church again after a long absence. We were so happy. The people around me became more important to me. My desire to share God's love with other people grew stronger. My life changed. Many of us got to know and understand each other better. Many take part in each other's lives and are there for each other. Fellowship has a completely new meaning. The 40 Days of prayer and worship by Dennis Smith was a great help to me. It is easier than it seems to find a prayer partner and to experience God. The people dear to us will thank us for it." Hildegard Welker, Crailsheim Seventh-Day Adventist Church, is a nurse on the surgical ward. (slightly shortened)

## JESUS OUR EXAMPLE

Jesus is our greatest example in all things. In Luke 3:21-22 NKJV we read: *"When all the people were baptized, it came to pass that Jesus also was baptized; and while He prayed, the heaven was opened. And the Holy Spirit descended in bodily form like a dove upon Him ..."*

Ellen White said the following about this event: "In response to His prayer to His Father, heaven was opened, and the Spirit descended like a dove and abode upon Him."[130]

It is amazing was happened during His ministry: "Morning by morning he communicated with his Father in heaven, **receiving from him daily a fresh baptism of the Holy Spirit.**"[131] If Jesus needed a fresh baptism of the Holy Spirit daily, then how much more do we need it!

---

130  E.G. White, *Ye Shall Receive Power* (1995), p. 14.4
131  E.G. White, *Signs of the Time*, Nov. 21, 1895

## CLOSING THOUGHTS

Through the Holy Ghost we have a wonderful leader in all life's situations and strength according to the riches of His glory.

Thus our characters can be changed and we can become valuable tools in God's work. Our daily surrender and baptism with the Holy Ghost will lead to a real breakthrough in our lives.

The Lord wants to prepare us for the greatest time in the world's history. He wants us to be personally ready for His coming and that in the power of the Holy Ghost we work together in completing the work of the gospel. He wants to lead us victoriously through difficult times.

Let God give you personal revival and reformation through daily surrender and a daily baptism with the Holy Ghost.

I want to close with a Bible text and a prayer for revival:

*"If my people ... will humble themselves, and pray and seek My face, and turn from their wicked ways, then I will hear from heaven, and will forgive their sin and heal their land."* (2 Chron. 7:14 NKJV)

*Prayer: Father in heaven, please give us humility (Micah 6:8). Put in our hearts a great desire to pray and seek Your face. Make us willing and help us to turn from our wicked ways. Please fulfill the prerequisites in us and as a result of Your promise let us hear Your answer. Forgive us for our sins and heal us from our lukewarmness and apostasy. Please help us to surrender ourselves to Jesus daily and by faith receive the Holy Ghost. Amen.*

**"A revival need be expected only in answer to prayer."** [132] **"The baptism of the Holy Ghost as on the day of Pentecost will lead to a revival of true religion and to the performance of many wonderful works."** [133]

---

132 E.G. White, *Selected Messages, Book 1* (1958), p. 121.1
133 E.G. White, *Selected Messages, Book 2* (1958), p. 57.1

# Abide in Jesus

Jesus Christ:
*"Abide in me, and I in you."*

HELMUT HAUBEIL

## *Abide in Jesus –*
## *Brochure 2 – Steps to personal revival*

### Chapter 1 – JESUS' MOST PRECIOUS GIFT

What does Jesus teach about the Holy Spirit?
Do you know Jesus' most impressive message?
What are the tasks of the Holy Spirit?

### Chapter 2 – SURRENDER TO JESUS

What does surrender mean? Do I consequently lose my own will?
Or will I become stronger?
What can prevent us from surrendering ourselves to Jesus?

### Chapter 3 – JESUS ABIDING IN YOU

What are the prerequisites for Jesus living in me?
How will "Christ abiding in me"
effect my life? The greatest achievement:
Experiencing the fullness of God.

### Chapter 4 – OBEDIENCE THROUGH JESUS

How can I live in joyful obedience?
What are the characteristics of faithful obedience?
Why is it a joy?

**Look at: www.steps-to-personal-revival.info**
There you can read it, download or sent to friends.
Scroll down. You find it after "Steps to Personal Revival".

## Recommendation for further Study

An important suggestion: read this booklet, if possible, every day for six days. Educational research has shown that it is necessary that such a vital topic for our life has to be read or heard six to ten times before a person can thoroughly understand it. Give it a try. The results will convince you.

A teacher tried it out: "These encouraging words captivated me: 'Try it at least once. The result will convince you.' I wanted to experience this and by the third reading it gripped me and I felt a great love for our Redeemer, which I had yearned for my whole life. Within two months I read the booklet six times and the result was worth it. It was as if I could understand what it was like when Jesus comes close to us and we can look into His pure, kind and loving eyes. From then on I never wanted to go without this joy for my Savior again." C.P.

I have received many thankful and enthusiastic testimonies about their new life with the Holy Ghost. Almost all of them were from readers, who intensively re-read the booklet multiple times.


## Literature on this Topic

- *40 Days [Book 1] Prayers and Devotions to Prepare for the Second Coming,* Dennis Smith, Review and Herald, 2009
- *40 Days [Book 2] Prayers and Devotions to Revive your Experience with God,* Dennis Smith, Review and Herald, 2011
- *40 Days [Book 3] God's Health Principles for His Last-Day People,* Dennis Smith, Review and Herald, 2011
- *40 Days [Book 4] Prayers and Devotions on Earth's Final Events,* Dennis Smith, Review and Herald 2013
- *If My People Pray – An Eleventh-Hour Call to Prayer and Revival,* Randy Maxwell, Pacific Press 1995
- *Revive Us Again,* Mark A. Finley, Pacific Press 2010
- *How to Be Filled With the Holy Spirit und Know it,* Garrie F. Williams, Review and Herald 1991
- *The Radical Prayer,* Derek J. Morris, Review and Herald 2008

## 40-DAYS INSTRUCTION MANUAL

You can find helpful material for organizing 40 Days of prayer with an evangelistic series afterwards using the 40 Day book by Dennis Smith on the website: *www.SpiritBaptism.org* under 40 Days Instruction Manual.

## New Experiences with living with the Holy Ghost

Our Lord Jesus said: *"But you shall receive power when the Holy Spirit has come upon you; and you shall be witnesses to Me ..."* (Acts 1:8 NKJV)

**A special request:** When you have experiences with living with the Holy Ghost in your personal life or when witnessing, then we would really appreciate it if you could send a short report to Helmut Haubeil so that he can share it in the *Missionsbrief* (a small newsletter in German on mission work). Please tell us if you only want your initials after the report or if we can share your full name and what church you attend. Please remember that your experience will strengthen others to grow in their walk with the Holy Spirit or to begin a journey with the Holy Spirit.

**Contact:**
Helmut Haubeil
Rosenheimerstr. 49
D-83043 Bad Aibling / Oberbayern, Germany
E-Mail: helmut@haubeil.net
Language: German or English